Adam Ochlenschläger

Axel and Valborg

A Tragedy in Five Acts

Adam Ochlenschläger

Axel and Valborg
A Tragedy in Five Acts

ISBN/EAN: 9783744717793

Printed in Europe, USA, Canada, Australia, Japan

Cover: Foto ©Thomas Meinert / pixelio.de

More available books at **www.hansebooks.com**

AXEL AND VALBORG

A Tragedy in Five Acts

AND OTHER POEMS

Translated from the Danish of Adam Oehlenschläger

BY

PIERCE BUTLER, M.A.
LATE RECTOR OF ULCOMBE, KENT

Edited by PROFESSOR PALMER, M.A., *St John's Coll., Cambridge*

With a Memoir of the Translator

LONDON
TRÜBNER & CO., 57 & 59 LUDGATE HILL
1874
[*All rights reserved*]

BIOGRAPHICAL SKETCH.

THE present translations are chosen from amongst several made by the late Rev. Pierce Butler, and left by him in an unfinished state. Mr Eiríkr Magnússon, of the University Library, Cambridge, has kindly revised the text, but the shorter poems are printed almost as the translator left them. The indulgence of the reader is craved for many literary faults in the latter, which would have been corrected had the manuscripts passed under the translator's final revision, but which might hardly be dealt with by another hand without injury to the spirit of the work.

These translations were made after a visit to Norway in 1856, which was the accomplishment of the desire of many years, and was succeeded by several others. This country had a peculiar interest for Pierce Butler as the cradle of his ancestors the "De Walters," of whom one had more than a thousand years before accompanied Rollo in his victorious expedition against Normandy. From Normandy another of the De Walters came to England with William the Conqueror, and here established the family, whence descend the present Marquis of Ormonde and Earl of Carrick. In 1177 the Chief-Butlership of Ireland was conferred on the representative of the family (whence the name), and the Butlers of Ireland have continued to hold this office for many generations.

The subject of our memoir was the fourth son of Lieut.-General the Hon. H. E. Butler. He graduated at Trinity College, Cambridge, in 1848, and soon afterwards took holy orders. In 1853 he accompanied his brother, Captain H. T. Butler, of the 55th Regiment, to Sinai. The latter had received leave of absence from Government for the purpose of exploring a part of the peninsula of Sinai, with the view of extending our knowledge of Biblical Geography; and at that time Pierce Butler conceived the idea of a future and more important expedition and survey. On the outbreak of the war in Russia, Captain Butler was recalled from Sinai, and fell at Inkermann; and another brother, James

Armar, the "hero of Silistria," died also of wounds received during that memorable siege—struck down in the height of a career so distinguished, that the sorrow felt at his death by his father and his friends was shared, as Lord Hardinge expressed it, "by the country, the army, and the sovereign."

Pierce Butler then determined to go out to Turkey, for the special purpose of volunteering his ministrations to the sick and wounded soldiers of our army. Such Christian service seemed the most fitting tribute he could pay to the memory of his lamented brothers. He accordingly proceeded to Constantinople in December 1854, and shortly afterwards accepted the offer of an appointment as one of the chaplains to our army in the Crimea. In discharging this duty, his gentle, genial manners and amiable disposition won the hearts of officers and men; and those now living who were with the Second Division in the camp before Sevastopol will ever retain a grateful recollection of his ministrations.

In 1861 he married, and settled at the family living of Ulcombe in Kent.

In 1867, encouraged by the assistance which Government had previously afforded towards the survey of Jerusalem, he resolved to make every effort to obtain, from amongst his own relations and friends, and other persons likely to take an interest in Biblical and geographical research, sufficient funds for a topographical survey of at least the most interesting parts of the peninsula of Sinai. In a few weeks he had received such promises of support from gentlemen interested in the subject that he felt justified in laying his plan before the Secretary of State for War. Sir John Pakington readily lent his aid, and at once authorised Sir Henry James to undertake the superintendence of the Sinai survey, as he had formerly that of the survey of Jerusalem, and to equip and send out a small party of officers and men of the Royal Engineers. Lord Stanley, as the head of the Foreign Office, also afforded the scheme every facility in his power, and Mr Butler, confident then of ultimate success, prepared to pay a short visit at once to Egypt, with the view of making arrangements for the arrival and progress of the surveying party, which it was proposed to despatch soon afterwards from this country, and which he himself hoped to accompany in their work. He had even taken his passage for Alexandria, and was actively preparing for departure, when severe illness overtook him; and on the 8th of February, 1868—on the very day, and almost at the very hour, on which he was to have started for Egypt—he died at his home in Kent, before he had quite completed his forty-second year.

AXEL AND VALBORG.

A TRAGEDY IN FIVE ACTS.

Persons.

HAKON HERDEBRED,* *King of Norway.*
SIGURD OF REINE, *his Marshal*
AXEL THORDSON, *his kinsman.*
VALBORG, *Axel's bride.*
WILHELM, *his friend.*
ERLAND, *Archbishop.*
KNUD, *Blackfriar.*
BJÖRN, *The Old.*
ENDRID, *a young man.*
KOLBEIN, *and several warriors.*
A HOSTILE WARRIOR, *with followers.*
GOTFRED, *Wilhelm's servant.*
QUEEN THORA, *with her ladies and maidens.*
BIARKEBEINER.
MONKS.

Date, 1162.

The action takes place in Christ Church in Nidaros. On both sides are tombs in the walls, in the middle of the pavement Harald Gille's tombstone. In the foreground are two massive columns supporting an arch; on the left are marked three crosses; the right displays the monogram

$$\cancel{\cancel{}}$$

surrounded by a wreath of forget-me-nots. Far in the background stands the high altar; over the altar-table is a golden shrine, which is illuminated by the painted windows in the choir, through which the sun is shining. In the centre of the nave is a corona.

* Broad-shouldered.

ACT I.

A

AXEL AND VALBORG.

A TRAGEDY IN FIVE ACTS.

ACT I.

AXEL.   WILHELM.

Wilhelm. So this, then, is the wide-known church of Trondhjem,
The fame whereof has reached to Rome itself?
Axel. And has fame bragged?
Wilhelm.   Nay, nay!
Axel.   Oh, what a temple!
Wilhelm. A mighty hollow-vaulted Dovre-field,
Axel. Here venerable quietude abides,
And sheds devotion in the tranquil mind.
Wilhelm. A glorious sight, as from mid-nave one looks
Up towards the altar.

Axel.   Mass is being sung
Within the choir. Hark, how the matins ring
Throughout the rounded arches of the church!
The waxen tapers in the brazen lustres
Shed down the solemn aisles their feeble rays;
'Tis like the gleam of hope in sorrowing heart.
Oh, what a sight! and see the early morning
Is glowing through the coloured window-panes.
All hail to thee, thou glorious rising sun!
Thou wak'nest all my childhood's memories.

    Wilhelm. But what can be yon golden chest I see
Above the altar?

    Axel.   'Tis Saint Olaf's shrine.

    Wilhelm. Ah, that is Olaf's shrine!

    Axel.   There are preserved
The sacred relics of the Saint of Norway.

    Wilhelm. Are still his beard and nails from time to time
Clipped by the kings?

    Axel.   Nay, Harald Haarderaade*
Thought it impious to disturb the corpse

           * Harold the Resolute.

In its last sacred rest. He therefore cast
Into the sea the keys of Olaf's shrine,
That so his noble dust might sleep in peace.
    Wilhelm (*looks at the columns*). Ha, by St Innocent! what rock-fast columns!
They have a stronger backbone, broader shoulders,
Than you and I; and they will tower aloft
When our tired limbs have long lain in the dust.
But what can these three crosses signify?
    Axel. Come, Wilhelm! let us see the other pillar.
    Wilhelm. But tell me first, what signify these crosses?
    Axel. They mark the height of Harald Haarderaade,
Of Olaf Kirre,* and of King Magnus.
But let us go and see the other pillar.
    Wilhelm. What would you look at?
    Axel.   A smaller effigy:
Not near so high,—not any giant's measure,—
No higher than a maid of fifteen years;
Not cut into the stone, but only scratched
With feeble lines upon the wooden frame.

    * Olaf the Quiet.

Wilhelm. Thy Valborg's measure?

Axel. Wait a moment yet!
Let me enhance the pleasure by delay.

Wilhelm. When did you carve it?

Axel. 'Twas five years ago,—
When to this church I came, to pray to God,
And bid a last farewell both to my love
And to my fatherland. Young Valborg's mother
Was lately dead, and Valborg in the convent
Was placed, to learn embroidery and reading.
She was but fifteen then ; but, O my brother !
Her ripened soul smiled with angelic sweetness
Through eyes of heavenly blue. Hither I came :
It was at morning's dawn. The day before
King Eistein had been seized and foully murdered.
Horror was driving me away from Norway.
Her sons waged cruel war against each other,
The land was filled with violence and blood,
While love was fighting fiercely in my breast.
I prayed to God to quench that mighty flame,
Which—innocent itself—full well I knew
Towards a kinswoman in guilt must burn.
I prayed : and while I prayed yon cloister-door,

Through which the pious sisters of the convent
Are wont to come to mass, was softly opened.
I wondered at their coming, for 'twas early.
But, ah! there was but one, and she a novice,
Whose loveliness no veil with cruel folds
Enshrouded yet. Closely the robe of black
Was fastened round her slender waist; her hair
Fell o'er her snow-white shoulders carelessly
In tresses soft as silk. She saw me not,
Wilhelm! She knelt before this very grave,—
Her mother's grave; and piously she raised
Her rounded arms, and clasped her lily-hands;
She prayed as I,—"O heaven! quench my love.
O mother! strengthen thou thy daughter's virtue!"
Then I forgot Saint Olaf,—all the saints,—
Aye, Heaven itself; for Heaven stood now revealed
Before mine eyes in Valborg. Never yet
Confession of my love had passed my lips.
As children they had called us man and wife:
It was in jest, because the darling girl
Already as a child was dear to me.
Now drew I near to her, my heart on fire
With courage kindled by the strongest love;

Now seemed to me all dangers past and gone.
My fate lay like a dragon at my feet;
Brave as Saint Michael did I stand upon it,
And strike my spear into the monster's back,
While my affection, like th' archangel's wings,
Rose towards the heavens. Before my Valborg thus
I stood: her graceful form encircled I
Boldly with my left arm, whilst with the right
I drew my sword, and sware by all the Saints,
Fair Valborg shall be Axel Thordson's bride
On earth, or else in yonder Heaven!

Wilhelm. Amen,
My gallant brother!

Axel. Ah! then trembled Valborg:
"What swearest thou, my Axel? Know'st thou not
All love like ours offends against religion?
Are we not kin? Doth not the Church forbid
Such marriages? Did not our mothers pray
Upon their death-beds earnestly to us
That we should quench this flame? Foretold they not
That nought but grief and ruin would await us,
If we should act in aught against their counsel?

Axel, behold our mothers on the tombstones!
How sorrowing they bow their heads, and weep
In tenderest compassion for us both,
Mourning their children's cruel destiny."
Then marked I our initials on yon pillar,
And sware again: "I come with dispensation
Home from the Pope,—or never, never more."

Wilhelm. Happy art thou to stand beside thy goal,
With all possessed which then was wanting.
Come, let us see the letters traced by thee.

Axel. Yes, that shall be the omen of my fate,

    [*He goes over to the pillar and discovers the wreath of flowers.*

O Wilhelm, Wilhelm! Valborg's true to me!
The sky is not so blue as these dear flowers.

    [*He embraces his friend.*

Wilhelm. O happy man! to love and to be loved.

Axel. Comrade! have patience with your friend, I pray,
Let not his weakness weary you. Soon, soon
The brightest joy of life will shine on Axel,
With Valborg, and his noble brother Wilhelm.

You came with me to Norway, here to learn
Our northern nature ; all shall you behold ;
But love is of our northern nature part.
Esteem and reverence for woman, Wilhelm !
The southern knights first learnt from northern
    warriors.
If you would learn the spirit and the life
Of northern lands, begin thou with our love.

 Wilhelm. Love on, good Axel ! Dream your
    happy dreams !
You chose an honest German for your friend,
And in his breast you ne'er shall fail to find
True sympathy in weal or woe.

 Axel.   I know it !
When Odin's hosts were parted, yet remained
Enough in speech and nature still to shew
Their common origin : and therefore ought
The Goth and German to be always friends.

 Wilhelm. In Henry's army you have shown your-
    self
As brave a knight, as now these memories
Of former days prove you a faithful lover.
I leave you, friend ! alone now with your love,

Whilst I shall go on board the ship, and give
Our men their orders.

   Axel.   True! I ought myself—

  Wilhelm. Nay, nay! you are excused. Leave it
     to me!
Thanks for your showing me the noble church.
On yonder seat you'll find the pilgrim-staff;
Beside it lies the pilgrim-cloak, in which
For the first time you see Valborg again.
And now I leave you, Axel! to your joy:
Meet me on board the ship whene'er you will.

   Axel. I will conduct you to the king, as soon—

  Wilhelm. First would I greet the bishop; but for
     this
There is no hurry, though there is for love.

                                [*He goes.*

   Axel. Brave Wilhelm! True and honourable
     heart!
My chosen friend, my trusty German comrade!
How brightly shines the sun of gladness now
Into my heart, as through the vaulted church,—
But see, what shadow comes to overcast
My morning glory? Ha, Blackfriar Knud!

I know him well: the same low, cunning glance
Is in his eye, the same deceitful smile
Upon his lip, as five years since. Could I
Escape him? But already he has seen me.
What if he tarries till my Valborg comes!
Ill-omened bird, must thou then be the first
To meet me here! 'Tis an unlucky sign!

   Knud (comes). O Holy Rood! what! what! Can I see right?

What? Axel Thordson? Axel in the land?
Do not mine eyes deceive me?

   Axel.   Nay, your eyes
See clear and true, my reverend father! Axel
Is here. God's peace! How fares it, brother Knud!

   Knud. God bless you, Axel! for this kindly greeting,
"How fares it?" The old way—the way of priests!
From cloister now to church, and then from church
Again to cloister, and at last from cloister
A step into the grave—such is monks' life.
But, my dear son! how fares it now with you?
Well, well! how stout and lusty you have grown!
Where have you journeyed? what have you been doing?

A stirring youth will see more in a year
Than all monks see together in their lives.
But what am I to think of your return?
                [*He observes Axel attentively.*

  Axel. Does it surprise you, father, that a Norseman
Should wish to see his Fatherland again?

  Knud. Wherefore you left our land I know full well:
Yes, all we monks had truly cause to praise
Resolve so pious in a youthful heart.
By absence you would try to overcome
Your sinful passion towards the beauteous Valborg:
Now that indeed was well done—right well done!
But your return to Norway, my dear son?—
But then, 'tis true, five years have passed away:
In five years much may be forgot, I know,
And in yon Roman lands are lovely women;
As lilies fair, as blooming as the rose,
As soft as doves, impassioned as the flame;
Pale northern beauty is forgotten there.
Is it not so, my son?

  Axel.   It may well be.

  Knud. Ay, ay! and so it was, I trow, with you;
And well it was, for 'twas a mortal sin

Your youthful heart at that time seemed to stand
In danger of committing.

Axel.   How fares Valborg?

Knud. Well, like young maids in general; she's grown
Pious, and good, and pretty.

Axel.   That she was
Already when I left.

Knud.   She promised well—
She promised well!

Axel.   Is she more beautiful?

Knud. That, my dear son! is not for me to judge.
A monk knows nothing about earthly beauty,
He looks upon the heavenly.

Axel.   And is Valborg
Still in the convent?

Knud.   Yes, from time to time;
But mostly with Queen Thora, Hakon's mother,
Up at the palace, where she soon will live.

Axel. How so?

Knud.   She's still indeed called "Axel's Bride"
In jesting 'mong the city girls; but then

We all well know that very soon King Hakon
Will share the crown of Norway with fair Valborg.

Axel. What? Hakon?

Knud. Why, he loves young Valborg
With all the passion of his heart.

Axel. And Valborg?

Knud. She—him in turn.

Axel. There liest thou, brother Knud!

Knud. Nay, nay, my youthful friend! I fully
thought
That you had piously o'ercome your sins.

Axel. She does not love King Hakon; nay, she
hates him.

Knud. Christ save us! hate the King!

Axel. And has he sued
For Valborg's hand?

Knud. Long since: and Valborg's kinsmen
All gave the king their "Yea."

Axel. But Valborg, monk!
But Valborg gave him "Nay."

Knud. She is brought up
In Christian piety; she knows obedience
Is always woman's chiefest ornament.

Axel. Nay, monk! By all the stars of Heaven!
    Valborg
Marries no Hakon, she is Axel's bride.
    Knud. And do you think indeed to perpetrate
A crime so foul?
    Axel.   Yea; my rightful bride
She shall become, by God and by my heart.
    Knud. But how?
    Axel.   Thereof the king and I must speak:
I owe to you no reckoning. Mine is Valborg,
In spite of all the devils—all'the monks.
                              [*He goes.*
    Knud. Important news! desirable for me!
A cause ecclesiastical; and one
With which th' archbishop will not like to meddle.
Once on a time he was in love himself,
Old fool! So, brother Knud! it seems that Axel
Will not renounce his Valborg with good-will,
In heat of love has he again forgot—
I must not lose a moment to reveal
All to the King. Erland is old and sick—
Another bishop must be thought of soon!
'Tis an important post, in times like these.

The King of Norway doubtless needs a man
Of strength and wisdom,—one who, by his deeds,
Has shown devotion.   Courage, Brother Knud!
Here is a glorious opportunity.
How can a lover recompense enough
The friend who gains for him his heart's desire?
Important news! desirable for me!   [*He goes.*
   Axel (*comes back in a pilgrim's cloak, fastened with
      mussel-shells; he has a white staff and a broad
      hat in his hand*).   Gone?—Hasten, if you
      please, to carry Hakon
The welcome news—I follow soon myself.
He to love her!—The king to love my Valborg!
No matter, she loves me—and whereby know'st—
And whereby know'st thou that she does love thee?
He is a king, and Valborg is a girl,—
And woman's lot is weakness.   Axel, shame!
Doubteth a sinner of an angel's virtue?
But girls are fond of show.   O Axel! Axel!
When here she knelt before her God—her soul
Glowing with sacred love—was't earthly show
That beamed from out those eyes of purity?
Ah, time wears all things out; it lays in ruins
Even the pyramids on Egypt's plains,

B

And how much more—O love ! thou surely art
No good and guileless passion, for thou wak'nest
Suspicion, hate, and fear within the heart !
Five years ! I too within that space have changed ;
I have not lost,—a warrior am I grown ;
Mine eye is calmer, keener than it was ;
My chin is covered with a thick dark beard ;
My sword has not grown rusty in its sheath
Meanwhile ; my deeds have won my leader's praise,
Henry the Lion ; for his sake I wear
Many a scar upon my breast and shoulders.
If I was deemed by Valborg worth her love
When but a boy, how much more as a man !
What loves a woman more than manliness ?

[*His eyes fall upon the wreath.*

Ah, lovely flowers ! like the beaming May-day,
Arched over by the blue of heaven, ye lighten
The sorrow in my heart. See, Thora comes
Returning from the matins with her maidens.
Now to the point ! In hoary sage's guise
I will spy out my fate. If Valborg fails me—
Away as quickly as I came ; like lightning
Back to the ranks of Henry's host, and there
Some Vendic axe will bring me longed-for-death ;

Or if the heathen offers, as a captive,
Me to his Radegast, his Svantevit,
His Provo, or unto the cruel Siva,—
What matter? I had fallen a sacrifice
Here to a Christian, and more cruel goddess.

> [*He steps aside. The Queen passes through the church with her ladies and maidens.*
>
> *Valborg (comes in the last pair: she stops in the foreground, and says to her companion)—*

Go on, Swanwhite! and leave me here alone,
That, after daily custom, I may pray
First at my father's and my mother's graves,
And I will follow soon.

> [*The Queen's attendants go. Valborg kneels down beside her parents' grave.*
>
> *Axel (who has returned in disguise, also kneels down at a little distance).* O heaven! 'tis Valborg!

I hardly know her. What majestic growth!
The whilom bud is now a full-blown rose.
How lovely is she grown! Her countenance
Is still the same: ah, no! the blushing roses
Have given place to sorrow's pallid lilies.

Yet I should shudder, if I saw her bloom
In joyous cheerfulness.

Valborg (rises up and looks around). I am alone:—
'Tis but an aged pilgrim who kneels yonder.

> [*She goes over to the pillar with the initials, takes off the wreath, and hangs on it a fresh one instead.*

I give thee my " Good morning," O my love!

Axel. O heaven!

Valborg (observes Axel). How piously the old man prays!

Axel. I thank thee, heavenly Father, for thy mercy!

Valborg. How blest his joy, the venerable man!
His sacred pilgrimage is ended now,
His heart is lightened of a heavy load;
Now stands he pure and guiltless by his grave,
Which opens for him as a friend's embrace.
O gracious God! how strange the course of life
Upon this earth! How often age enjoys
A childlike gladness, while the youthful heart
Must pine away in dark and hopeless sorrow.

> [*She goes towards him, whilst he rises.*

All hail, all bliss to thee, my pious pilgrim!

Axel. My thanks are due to you, fair lady Valborg !
Valborg. Thou knowest me ?
Axel.   To Nidaros I journeyed,
Partly to kneel before St Olaf's shrine,
Partly to bring a letter and a greeting
To thee from Germany, wherethrough I wand'rd.
Thy cousin Helfred have I visited
At Immersborg : and she foretold I'd have
A welcome cheer for this my joyful message.
   Valborg. I'm known to none throughout the wide,
       wide world
But Lady Helfred, trusty friend of mine.
But coming from afar,—what tidings canst thou bring ?
   Axel. The lady has a brother.
   Valborg (blushes).   Axel Thordson ?
   Axel (aside). Ye pallid flowers ! changing now again
To roses !—(*aloud.*) Right, fair lady ! Axel Thord-
      son—
A warrior brave, though somewhat sad of mood.
In Saxony, in Henry's camp, I met him.
No sooner had he learnt that I was bound
For Norway, than he handed me this letter,
And bade me give it into thine own hand.

Valborg (casts a timid side glance through the church: when she sees that she is alone with the stranger, she takes the letter, and says)—

Old man! thou bringest me a welcome message.

Axel. Do I? May God in heaven then bless thee for it!

Valborg. You take an interest in Axel's fate?

Axel. And in fair Valborg's too. But read the letter!

Valborg (opens the letter and reads)—

"Young Axel doth this letter write,
    Valborg, thou sweetest maiden!
Christ grant that it may reach thy sight,
    With Axel's true love laden.

This ring comes from my hand to thee,
    Thy finger wear it ever;
At heart I love thee faithfully,
    And can forget thee never.

Remember thou, my youthful bride,
    That thus our troth is plighted;
Though Axel wander far and wide,
    'Mid foreign folk benighted.

Henry the Lion is his lord;
    His golden spurs gleam brightly,
And brightly his Italian sword,—
    For Axel's rank is knightly.

But ah! sweet sleep he cannot find
   After the fight is ended;
Strange visions haunt his troubled mind
   With thy loved image blended.

O Valborg! be thou true to me!
   Forget not our loves' story!
For all the world I fail not thee,
   My joy, my pride, my glory!

Our evil fortune soon may change
   And end our days of sadness,
And Axel bring thee tidings strange
   To fill thy heart with gladness;

And he may stand before thy sight,—
   Believe it scarce thou darest?
Farewell now, Valborg,—lily white,
   Of all fair flowers the fairest!"

[*Valborg gazes mournfully on the letter, and repeats slowly and despairingly*—

"And he may stand before thy sight,—
   Believe it scarce thou darest?"

[*She raises her eyes, and at the same moment becomes aware of Axel, who had thrown off the pilgrim's cloak.*

O heaven!

   Axel (*in her arms*)—

"Here is he, Valborg!—lily white,
   Of all fair flowers the fairest!"

Valborg.   Axel !

Axel.   Valborg !

Valborg.   Christ Maria !
Is it thyself ?

Axel.   Oh no, it is not Axel ;
For Axel was a sad and silent youth,—
And now thy snow-white arms, fair Valborg, clasp
The happiest and most prosperous of knights.

Valborg. My Axel ! is it possible ?

Axel.   Sweet maid !
All things are possible to faithful hearts,
And in all things thy pilgrim has succeeded.
He stands beside his goal, and not his grave,
And thanks our heavenly Father for His mercy.
I sware an oath that I would ne'er return
Until the Church had giv'n us leave to love.
See here the Holy Father's dispensation !
Now can we love, my Valborg ! without sin.
The precious deed I carry in a cover
Of silk upon my heart.   A heaven's letter
That yellow parchment is !   Read !   " Hadrianus
Episcopus, servus servorum Dei "—
Ah ! I forgot, 'tis in the Latin tongue—

But it allows thee to return my love ;—
The worthy old man sware me that. And now
Swear thou, I pray, beloved of my heart!
On this broad tombstone, under which doth rest
The dust of our forefather Harald Gille,
That thou to-day wilt kneel before yon altar,
With Axel as thy bridegroom.

  Valborg.   Oh, my Axel!
Thou know'st not that the king—

  Axel.   All know I,—all!
He loveth thee!—and thou?

  Valborg.   And I love Axel.

  Axel. O sweetly-sounding, heaven-taught eloquence!
Say it once more,—oh say it yet once more,
Thou lovely lily-wand!—I did not hear
The first time what thy rose-bud lips did speak.

  Valborg. Valborg loves Axel.

  Axel.   Have ye heard it, walls?
Ye lofty arches! altars of the Lord!
Valborg loves Axel!—Now but death itself
Shall ever part thee from him. Valborg, come—
Come let me place this ring upon thy finger!
            [*He loses it.*

'Tis fallen !

Valborg.   O God !

Axel.   It rolled into a crevice.

Valborg. 'Tis fallen into Harald Gille's grave.

Axel. Ten better shall be wrought, for every one
Of Valborg's slender, alabaster fingers.
With strings of pearl her hair shall be adorned ;
Rich silk, with roses and with lilies broidered,
Shall deck her bosom ; and her tiny feet
Shall be enclosed in silver-buckled shoes.
The train of thy red mantle shall be borne
By pages, whensoe'er, as Axel's wife,
Thou goest to the church from Axel's court.
Enough rich gold from Vendish carven gods
Fell to thy true knight's lot.   Thou wast his shield-
    maid,
My stately Valborg !

Valborg.   O beloved youth !
How wonderfully art thou also changed :
Only thy heart, thy love, are still the same.
I hardly can discern thy roguish dimple
Here in thy chin, for all these thick black curls,—
Barbarian thou art grown !   Why, Valborg loved

A fair and smooth-faced youth; now she embraces
A sun-burnt, bearded savage of the wilds.

Axel. And as a proof that thou art not afraid
Of this rude savage with the thick black beard,
Come, press thy face so smooth, so silky-soft
Against this swarthy down, whilst with thy mouth
The first sweet seal of thine unaltered love
Thou dost impress on Axel's lips.

                                  [*He kisses her.*

Valborg.   My Axel!

Axel. My Valborg!—So!—Now will I go to
    Hakon;
Now have I drunk a draught of strength and courage.
I do not fear: he shall not rob me of
My bride:—nay, more, he cannot, for he is
A northern chief, and he will not be base:—
It is my duty to believe his honour.
Farewell!—Ah me, how hard it is for Axel
To tear himself from his beloved one!
But it must be. Soon shall we be united
As close as our initials on the column.
See, sweetest maiden! what is yonder "A?"
A "V" reversed; and what is yonder "V?"

An " A " reversed. So is it with our hearts :
We are one soul,—now rent indeed in twain,
But ever striving to be one again.
Christ bless thee! Deck thee as a bride. Thou findest
Thine Axel here again as bridegroom.

[*He goes.*

Valborg. Axel!
How he has grown in manliness and courage!
With joyous confidence his eye is beaming.
Why go away, and leave thy Valborg here
Alone behind, amid the tombs, my Axel?
And now again her eyes turn anxiously
Towards the pallid image of her mother.
She still weeps mournfully : ah, 'tis as though
She were about to say—" Unhappy ones!
Ye are rejoicing in a short-lived hope :
But cruel fate has raised an iron wall
Between your youthful hearts. First in the grave"—
O God! 'tis in the grave his ring has fallen,—
In Harald's grave. There stands he in his armour—
The monarch dead—so fierce and terrible,
The hand on sword, with wrathful-knitted brow.
Oh be not wroth with us, great ancestor!

Mine Axel brings the papal dispensation :
Our marriage now no longer is a crime.
But ah ! unmoved by me, he threatens still.
And Axel's ring—O all ye saints in heaven !
'Tis fallen into our forefather's grave.

                                        [*She goes.*

ACT II.

ACT II.

King HAKON.   SIGURD OF REINE.

Sigurd. All hail to thee, my lord and master
    Hakon!—
Tis plain to see that one must go to church,
If now-a-days one would be sure to find
The King of Norway.
    Hakon.   Do you bring us tidings?
Have you procured us news of Erling, Sigurd?
    Sigurd. A merchant ship has run into the Fjord,
That under cover of the night had crept
Away from Bergen:—it brings evil tidings.
In southern Norway is young Magnus chosen,
And Erling rages wild in Bergen. Slain
Is Arne Brigdeskal, your steward, sire,
And likewise Ingebiorn, the governor.
All merchant vessels are detained in Bergen,
Lest they should bring you word to Nidaros

Of Erling's preparations.   Accident
Have we alone to thank for this last news.

Hakon. The traitor wishes one such other greeting
As Inge got on board the *Bekesud.**

Sigurd. No prudent man will e'er despise his foe.
Such chances are not always found, as when
Upon the ice you met Gregorius Dagson ;
And Erling is no fool, such as King Inge,
The weakly withered-foot : from childhood has
He learnt to bear the steel.   In Niorfasund †
The axe-stroke of the negro had not power
To slay him, when with Ragnvald Jarl he sailed
To Saerkland,‡ and upon the voyage boarded
The haughty Dromund.§   Ever since that blow
He holds his head upon one side, and so
He is called " Erling Skakke." ‖

Hakon.   We will try
To strike at him upon the other side :—
So goes it, think I.

Sigurd.   May God grant it, sire !

---
* Name of a man-of-war.   † Straits of Gibraltar.
§ Land of the Saracens.
‡ A kind of Levantine merchant vessel, and sometimes man-of-war.
‖ Skakke, askew.

But, king! forgive an old man's hardihood :—
What dost thou here among the graves? why sighest
Thou like a weakly girl? Why doth thy cheek
Turn pale? why glows thine eye with sickly light
As doth the drunkard's? Hakon! can a maiden
So rob thee of thy spirit and thy strength?—
Look you, the nation needs a valiant chief,
Who will combine the strength of Haarderaade
With Magnus' wisdom. Thou possessest now
The throne of Norway, for the kingdom's heirs
Are fallen; and right has claimed for thee the sceptre,
As Harald Gille's last remaining grandson.
Another race is rising now, once more
To waste the nation's blood in civil war :—
Hakon! the hope of Norway rests on thee.
Has not King Valdemar in Denmark shown
How, by the hero, strife's soon turned to order?

 Hakon. You give me then th' example of my foe?

 Sigurd. Follow his virtues, and avoid his faults!
But go not dreaming thus within these walls,
The haughty tokens of Augustine's pride.
Now is he building other walls in Bergen
Against thy power, to Erling Skakke's profit.

Hakon. Be not uneasy, Sigurd! soon my longing
Shall find its object.

Sigurd. Well then, lose no time!
Let it be quickly done; appease your longing;
Shake off the dreaming youth, the sighing lover,
And head your warriors like a chief and hero.

Hakon. As heroes we will stand prepared for Erling.

Sigurd. It is full time, then, that you think upon it,
For what secures you 'gainst the attack of Erling?
Gather your ships, and let the trumpet's blast
Be heard to-day! Set warlike pipes a-sounding,
Buckle your armour on, and show yourself
A valiant chieftain, able to subdue
Thy traitor foes.

Hakon. Yes, yes,—to-morrow, Sigurd!
To-morrow. 'Tis impossible to-day.

Sigurd. Yet more impossible perhaps to-morrow,
If Erling should attack us in the night.
Forget not—

Hakon. And forget not your respect!

Sigurd. 'Twas simple faithfulness that made me
    speak.
It grieves me sore that Erling is believed,

Because ill-luck confirms his slanderous rumours.
Tradition saith, indeed, that Harald Gille
By treachery obtained the crown of Norway:
For this ('tis said), and for the cruelty
He showed towards Magnus Blind, Bishop Reinald,
It goes so ill with his posterity;
And luck and thriving can there never be
With all the Gille race, whate'er it does.
So saith the people, and it grieves me sore.

 Hakon. Such idle tales as these may grieve old crones,
But not old warriors.

 Sigurd.   Yet such traditions
Are venerable.

 Hakon.   Superstitious too.
But here comes Brother Knud!

 Sigurd.   In him at least
Is nothing venerable. Hypocrite!
How I do loathe the sight of yon black snail.
Come, Sire! with me, and leave the snail to crawl.

 Hakon. Talk reverently of the king's confessor.

 Sigurd. He your confessor?—In the name of God!

 Hakon. I have a weighty matter to confide to him.

Sigurd. God help thy case then! Farewell! I am not
In general so lightly put to flight,
But with black devils Sigurd is a coward.

[*He goes.*

Hakon. Unbearable,—with all his honesty,
With all his power!—a never-ending scold.
It tickles Sigurd's sense of vanity
To rant and rate whene'er he sees in others
A craving which he does not feel himself.
Thy joy is all in war,—and therefore Hakon
Must take delight in war alone; thine age
Has quenched the fire of love,—and therefore Hakon
Must also quench love's flame within his heart.
How wise! The icy winter with its snows
Upbraids the spring that it is decked with flowers.
Nay, love I will; and love with all the strength
My youthful heart can feel. Behold thou then
My kingdom here in Nidaros,—in Bergen,—
In Vigen,—where thou wilt :—I see it only
In Valborg's heart; and that shall never Erling
Bereave me of, whene'er my true affection
Has gained for me possession of my throne.

[*To the monk, who stands at a respectful distance.*

Come nearer! Come, good Brother Knud! Old Sigurd
Is gone away.

Knud.   I was indeed amazed
To see him here: he has not been in church
These twenty years.

Hakon.   Say, have you found young Valborg?
Have you by sound advice endeavoured to——

Knud. "Endeavoured?"—ah, my king! in general
Can good advice accomplish much, I know:
But true advice is wasted here,—the more——

Hakon. What then?

Knud.   You know the childish whim,—the love
That never could be banished from her mind!

Hakon. Can you not paint it in such hideous hues,
With all the reddest colours of hell-flames,
That it will frighten her? Can you not, besides,
Prove to her, by convincing argument,
That such a lover, out of sight so long,
Must either have been faithless, or be dead?

Knud. It is no easy matter to dispute
With women, sire!—and more especially

When love is strong. No argument avails;
No time, no place is thought of any moment:
The lover still seems present, even though
He were on service 'mong the Vaerings, with
Kyrialax* in Greece——

Hakon. O cruel fate!

Knud. And how much more, when suddenly he comes
To Nidaros?

Hakon. What say'st thou?

Knud. I say this—
How much more so, when suddenly he comes
To Nidaros?

Hakon. To Nidaros?

Knud. So called
King Olaf Trygvason, your forefather,
Our good old town.

Hakon. Ha, monk!

Knud. Forgive me, king!
I surely thought they had already told you
That Axel Thordson is come back again.

Hakon. Come back again?

* Northern corruption of Kyrios Alexios.

Knud. What? know you not? Forgive
That I unwittingly have been the first
To bring unwelcome tidings.

Hakon. Axel here?

Knud. He seeks you everywhere, my lord and king!

Hakon. Have all the powers of evil then combined?
What? Axel here?—and thinks he still the same
Of Valborg?

Knud. "Thinks," your Majesty?—aha!
When thinks a lover? Nay, like Hekla's fire,
So burns he fiercely for her soft embrace.

Hakon. Now shall we see which of us two will win
This game of chess.

Knud. Then, sire! guard you the king
Against the pawn. By quietness and prudence
The game may still be won,—the queen preserved.
Will you permit me to speak out my mind?

Hakon. Speak!

Knud. Axel is a dreamer now as ever.
In Germany he long has roamed about,
Staking his luck on many a rash adventure
With Henry's army; and the German lord
Has by a word aroused his youthful spirit.

Now is he swollen with self-confidence,
And deems that all he takes in hand must prosper.
The aged Hadrian has now exchanged
This earthly life for immortality;
And Victor now contests with Alexander
The popedom. Alexander by the council
Was chosen, it is true; but Frederic Redbeard,
In spite of this, supports the claim of Victor.
There's nought but war and tumult: Henry marches
Against the Vends, Frederic to Italy:
In Denmark and in Norway long have raged
Murder and violence and civil strife.
The haughty knights are turning this to profit;
For ever, as the royal power sinks,
Riseth each knight in strength proportionate.
They think, and say, that popes and princes too,
With their own business have enough on hand,
And so that each may do as seems him good;
And such a moment Axel seizes on.

 Hakon. As sure as I am king——
 Knud.   Your Majesty!
You have permitted me to speak my mind,
I pray you therefore for a gracious ear,

Till I have spoken all.   Your Majesty
Loves Valborg—naturally ! she is fair ;
And you hate Axel Thordson—naturally !
He is the favoured one.   Your Majesty
Expects to gain the victory—naturally !
You are the powerful one.   So far is all
Proper, and orderly, and natural.
Now go we further.   Home comes Axel Thordson,
And sues for Valborg's hand.   But, look you ! Valborg
Is fatherless and motherless.   As king
You stand to Valborg in a father's stead.
To you the youth must sue for Valborg's hand,—
A hand which, on aforenamed excellent,
Most natural, indisputable grounds,
You will not give him.   Here there is no need
Of any game ; our cause goes steadily
Its legal, crooked course ;—a course that surely
Will issue to the profit of the king,
And here your Majesty will have no need
To lay aside your royal dignity
In angry strife of words, or otherwise.
Young Axel will approach you as a subject,
And lay before you, with due reverence,

His errand.   Doubtless, since he now is come
To Nidaros, will Axel make his king
The offer of his sword 'gainst Erling 'Skew :—
Of course the offer will not be refused.
Then goes he further, and seeks Valborg's hand,—
That is a cause ecclesiastical.
You send him to the priests.   I fetch the book,—
I prove his blood-relationship with Valborg ;
The old archbishop's duty forces him
To stop the marriage, though indeed his will
Be most reluctant.   So the matter ends.
The king's calm dignity is undisturbed,
And yet his object is attained.

 Hakon.   I feel
How different from Sigurd's haughty rudeness
Are your most wise and friendly words of counsel,
My dear confessor !—yes, so shall it be !
Man ever strives to seize on happiness,
And uses every means that nature's self
Has stamped with mark of lawfulness !   *His* love
Offends against the Church—against good manners,
But *mine* is innocent, and therefore Heaven
Will surely take its part.   Go, fetch the book !

Do not delay to bring it, Friar Knud!

[*Knud goes.*

In this was Sigurd right,—it ill beseems
The King of Norway to sigh out his life,
Consumed by ceaseless longings. She shall be
My queen, whether she will or will not. Ha!
A maid is like a child : it cries for that
Which wisdom's hand withholds, but soon forgets
Its little grief, and thanks the prudent care
That forced it to its real happiness.
Is Hakon not a handsome well-grown man—
Young, active, spirited ? Is he not king?
Is he not king, too, over Throndhjem's men,—
So proud a people, that one might believe
It would be ruled alone by God in heaven?
Yes,—Valborg shall be mine! But see I right?
Control thyself, my wrath! Swell not, my heart!

 Axel (*comes*). All hail to thee, King Hakon Herdebred!

 Hakon. Be welcome, Axel! I had heard already
Of your arrival.

 Axel.   I was told that here
I should find you ; and——

Hakon.   Welcome, kinsman, back!
Be welcome! But to what must we ascribe
The happiness of seeing you again?
We all believed young Axel had become
A knight of such renown with German Henry,
That he had clean forgotten poor old Norway.

Axel. Norsemen and Danes are not so readily
Forgetful of their fatherland. The Norseman
Full oft roams far and, wide in foreign lands,
But to the dear-loved fatherland again
His wandering steps return; or else he takes
His fatherland away with him, and founds
Another Denmark or a Norway,—now
In England, now in France, or Italy,—
Wherever chance may take him.

Hakon.   Many a hero
Has left his country at a time when peace
Was wearying him at home; or else when flood,
When pest, or famine drove him from his hearth.
With you it was far otherwise; you went
When bloody swords were clashing 'gainst each other,
When there was honourable work to do
For any warrior. Therefore must one judge

That to your fatherland you had preferred
A foreign land.

Axel. My fatherland !—and what
Is fatherland,—and what are brother-subjects,—
When madness and ambition fiercely burn
Through every vein, and rage around its heart?
What is a subject's, what a warrior's duty,
When every tie of duty is unloosed?
He is a craven, who through good and ill
Will not stand by his rightful sovereign
With life and blood; but what can warrior do
When four kings struggle for the mastery,
And all with equal right, and brothers all,
Though savage all as tigers 'gainst each other?
My father, Thord Husfreyja, was your father's,
King Sigurd's, honourable, faithful man.
He fought and fell with him. When Eistein came
From Scotland, and took pity on your youth,
And held the throne of Throndhjem after Sigurd.
I served him faithfully, until he fell
Into King Inge's hands, and shamefully
Was hewn across the back with heavy axe-strokes,
While with his pallid lips he bit the grass.

Now Inge was sole king, and could I then
Remain? Could I swear Inge fealty? fealty
To him, your father's murderer? I fled,
Horror without, and heartfelt grief within.
But now is fate more mild; and Eistein's host
Has chosen you, and you have slain King Inge.
Now you are rightful lord of Throndhjem's men,
And I am here again, to offer you,
As Throndhjemer, and warrior, and kinsman,
My strong right hand against your haughty foes.

 Hakon. This long while, Axel! have you been the friend
Of Denmark's Valdemar, mine enemy.

 Axel. When I knew Valdemar he was not so:
He was a valiant, noble-minded hero;—
That is he still. I offered him mine arm,
When he, in spite of craft and treachery,
Was 'stablishing his power in his own realm.

 Hakon. In his own realm? You mean in Barbarossa's:
Has he not taken Denmark as a fief,
Dependent on the German empire?

 Axel.   Nay!

That was a feint, concerning only Venden.
Frederick by stratagem enticed him to
St Jean de Laune, and made him take his hand :
And all the world laughed at the Emperor's
Vain-glorious subtlety.   But Valdemar
In Germany so highly was esteemed,
That mothers met him at the cities' gates,
Holding their children up to him to touch,
That they might have good luck in after life ;
While on his march the peasants prayed him take
A handful of their corn and scatter it,
That so their seed might have the more increase.

Hakon. And such an emperor you served?

Axel. I served
Henry the Lion, Duke of Saxony.

Hakon. I lately heard an anecdote of him
Which took my fancy, and which shows he is
Not only (as we know) a valiant hero,
But, what is more, a conscientious Christian.
He has allowed to be divorced from him
His wife Clementia, because they were
Too near of kin.

Axel. Nay, that was not the ground.

D

Henry the Lion is a warrior; he
Would found a powerful princely race; his wife
Bare him no sons,—that was the real cause.
That this takes not my fancy, you will see,
I do not doubt, King Hakon! since you know
That I love one who is of kin to me;
And I am sure you would not wish to hinder
My happiness and hers.

 Hakon.   Is 't possible?
Have you not yet forgot that boyish folly?

 Axel. So little, that I hope this very day,
With your permission, to make Valborg mine
At yonder altar.

 Hakon.   You are hasty, Axel!

 Axel. So can the lover scarce be called, who truly
Has waited for his bride through five long years.

 Hakon. Your bride?—and is it then so very certain
That Valborg loves you?

 Axel.   See you yonder wreath
Around our names? That wreath has Valborg woven.
Five summers now the field has given its flowers
Each morn for such a wreath, to be entwined
By Valborg's snow-white hands.

Hakon.   And those initials?
Axel. Has Axel graven.
Hakon.   Yonder wreath of flowers?
Axel. Has Valborg woven.
Hakon.   Ha!
Axel.   Nay, hear me, sire!
I see your eye is gleaming, and I know
Your inmost feeling. Speak we honestly,
As Norsemen should, of what concerns our hearts.
To me it is impossible to feign:
I still love Valborg—Valborg still loves me.
See, Hakon! you are ruler of a realm—
A great, and proud, and noble warrior race:
Would you then rob an honourable kinsman
Of all he has in life—his bride betrothed?
O chief! your honour calls you, and your birth
Beckons to noble deeds. 'Tis not yet time
For peaceful love: such is your Norna's judgment,—
She summons you to Hilda's game. Arise,
Follow her leading! Arm against the foes,
And crush the opposition, that would shake
Your throne beneath you. Many a valiant man
Will follow you, and with the very blood

Of Axel's heart will he repay to you
Your goodness,—if you give him back his Valborg.

   Hakon. Kinsman ! your words disclose your state
      of mind.
Emotions the most widely different
Rise in your heart within a moment's space.
A suitor for a maid you come, whilst you
Present yourself as warrior to your king.
You give me counsel, like a wise old man ;
Then, as a timid and impetuous youth,
Take refuge in the goodness of my heart.
Content yourself, that Hakon calm and cold
Meets you with dignity, and in due order
Answers the wild confusion of your speech.
You offered me your sword, if I mistake not,
And fealty, as a native Throndhjemer,—
To me, your rightful king, 'gainst Erling Skakke?

   Axel. I offer it in all sincerity.

   Hakon. And in like manner this your worthy offer
Do I accept.

   Axel.   Then, sire ! this hand-grasp makes
Axel your faithful and unfailing man.

   Hakon. I thank you, and I value high your worth.

Now as regards the other things,—about
That fire of love you think you see in me,
The cruelty that frightened you, and so forth,—
All that you say my dignity must take
As flowing from a want of reverence, if
Your passion were unknown to me. Young Valborg
Is fatherless and motherless—forsaken :
My royal power alone is her protection.
Now, if the king, by sharing Norway's crown
With such a lovely being, should reward
A virtue that is worthy of that crown ;
If he thereby should do his best to quench
A love accounted sinful by the Church,
And cause her, by his tenderness, to lose
All memory of a lover, long unseen,—
Were that a crime?

Axel.   O noble Hakon ! now
I understand you :—as a king you would—
A fatherly protector—safely guard
The lovely maid, and cheer her lovely life.
You did not love her, and so all is well !
That very generosity of soul
Which urged you heretofore to wed young Valborg,

Will cause you doubtless to renounce your purpose
When Axel comes, and Valborg's happiness
Depends upon her union with her lover.

Hakon. You talk for ever like a drunken man!
I do not love? and wherefore not? and whence
Have you discovered this? Are you alone
Able to see the gracious charms of Valborg?
And can a hero feel no fire of love
Because he blusters not as wild as you?

Axel. And do you then love Valborg?

Hakon.   As a man,
And as a king. I wish her real welfare,
Therefore I wish her marriage to be founded
On lawfulness and innocence. Besides,
I think that I can render Valborg's life
As happy and as prosperous as you.

Axel. The loving heart can see no joy in life,
Save in the object of its choice.

Hakon.   You think
Yourself the chosen one?

Axel.   Let Valborg judge
Betwixt us in this cause. As noble knight,
Honour a woman's will; and as a king,

Respect your subjects' rights; and as a Christian,
Forget not what is told of Naboth's vineyard.

Hakon. I will not act with arbitrary power:
But Valborg cannot judge betwixt us here;
For by the law a maiden is a ward,
And therefore cannot judge in her own cause.
Axel! the Holy Church must judge betwixt us.

Axel. Therewith am I content.

Hakon. Think not that Hakon
Will act a tyrant's part; yet neither think
Him fool enough to throw away a prize
From which the Church's law excludes his rival.

Axel. Is that your real meaning, and your purpose?

Hakon. So help me Olaf, mine elected saint!

Axel. For such a purpose has an upright man
No need to fear, and love no cause to mourn.
On Christian duty your demand is founded;
'Tis a demand I made upon myself.
'Tis therefore Valborg has not seen her Axel
This many a weary year; nor ever had
She seen him, noble Hakon! had not God,
The sure protector of all faithful love,
Opened at length a way for him to Valborg,

E'en through the sacred arches of the Church.

Hakon. What is 't you say?

Axel. I give into your hands
The gracious letter of Pope Hadrian :
It is a copy,—that he wrote himself,
Already has been sent to the archbishop.
This bull annuls my kinship with fair Valborg;
Our marriage therefore is no longer crime.

Hakon (*with an outburst of passion*). Ha, treachery!
—O hell!

Axel. And can it be
King Hakon Herdebred has laid on Axel
A fair condition, with a secret purpose
That it should never be fulfilled by him?

Hakon. Away from out my sight!

Axel. O Hakon, Hakon!

Hakon. Away, I say! and do not longer dare,
A subject as you are, presumptuously
To put my long-forbearance to the test.

Axel. I am a scion of the Gille root
As well as you; I am a knight renowned
In Henry's host; and now I am your warrior,
But not your slave. Young Valborg is my bride :

Your might may not invade the Church's shrine.
I go and bring her to the holy altar.
Compose yourself; subdue your raging passion,—
The noblest victory for any hero.

   Hakon. Away, I say!

   Axel. Let God then be our judge!   [*He goes.*

   Hakon. Is this the end of all my darling dreams?—
It is thy fate, King Hakon Herdebred!
One comes to rob thee of thy very realm,
Another comes to rob thee of thy bride.
What is there more to rob thee of?—ah, yes!
A heart enraged.   But such a robbery
Were not so light.   'Tis bursting with revenge,
'Tis thirsting after blood,—my wrathful heart.

   [*He becomes aware of Brother Knud, who has come in
      at the close of the foregoing scene, has laid down
      the church book, and reads most attentively the
      parchment which Hakon had let fall.*

What wilt thou, monk?

   Knud (*quietly, without raising his eyes from the
      parchment*). Permits your Majesty—

   Hakon (*gazes wrathfully at the wreath and initials,
      draws his sword, and cuts them away with a*

large chip from the pillar). Well done, my
    trusty blade! In such wise shalt
Thou cut in twain the knot that binds together
My sole possession with this worthless villain.
How slily he contrived to twist the matter,
To draw the word he wanted from my lips.
But stay, thou traitor! Nay, thy treacherous cunning
Shall not avail thee: thou shalt never press
The fair one to thy heart, as long as this
My head is over ground;—that do I swear
By Norway's crown!

    Knud (*still reading with evident joy*). But if your
    Majesty—

    Hakon. Off with your book, and hold your prating
    tongue!
It ill beseems a monk with cunning speech
To smooth the way to happiness. A king
Should use his power. And, by my majesty,
That will I! Think you Hakon, as a boy,
Will hold the taper for you at the altar,
And light you with it to your bridal bed?
With roses shall your bridal bed be decked,
With blood-red sheets, and pillows brimstone-blue.

The signal has been given.—What wilt thou, monk?

Knud (*who has finished reading*). Permit me with a
    word, your Majesty——

Hakon. Peace, miserable man! I will no longer
Pine here among the tombs; I will no more
Waste precious time in gossiping with monks,
Nor dream, good Sigurd!—that I promise thee.
I will shake off the lover, and enjoy
My pleasure like a man; and meet thee too
As hero, valiant Sigurd! and as king.
                            [*He hastens away.*

Knud. Wild as a wolf.—But hear, King Hakon!
    hear!
The bull from first to last is without force:
The chief thing is forgotten. Hear me, sire!
                            [*He makes after the king.*

ACT III.

ACT III.

Archbishop ERLAND. KNUD, *with the church book.*

Knud. Forgive, most reverend father! that I dare
To interrupt your converse with the canons,
But duty calls; you must prepare yourself
At once: young Axel hastens with his marriage.
We may expect the bridal company
At any moment,—it has left the castle.
    Erland. Hath Heaven vouchsafed me ere my death this joy,
To join together two such noble hearts?
    Knud. It grieves me sorely that I must so soon
Disturb, most reverend father! this your joy.
But what the world calls Fate, the wise man deems
To be the hand of God; and so no doubt
You will submit yourself to Heaven's high will,

When you have understood that Axel's marriage
Has not found grace and favour, and somehow,
By reason of a most strange circumstance,
The dispensation, which Pope Hadrian
Had granted Axel, has no force at all.

Erland. As surely as the Holy Church's arm
Extends beyond the king's, so surely shall
This bull in all its fulness be confirmed.

Knud. The bull, most reverend father! has no
force.

Erland. But has not Hadrian, in words express,
Annulled young Axel's kinship with fair Valborg?

Knud. Quite true, archbishop! I have also read
The bull entire; and I have not forgotten
My Latin altogether, so that I
Have understood each word. Relationship
'Twixt Axel and fair Valborg is annulled—
That is to say, relationship as kin,
As cousins——

Erland. Well, and is not that enough?

Knud. It ought to seem so. Axel Thordson, too,
Undoubtedly supposed it was enough;
For otherwise I cannot understand

How he could ever pass a matter by,
Of equal moment with their kinship; but
'Tis like he did not know of it himself.
[Erland starts.
As cousins truly they may love each other,
But as twin children of baptismal birth
The Church forbids their marriage still.
 Erland.   What sayest thou?
 Knud. Truth, which the church's book shall testify,
Most reverend father! you had lately come
To fill the post deserted by Augustine;
And therefore are you not so well informed
Of all that to our Church relates, as one
Whose life has passed between these convent walls.
Your life has raised you to the bishopric:
One used to think indeed, that worthily
To wield the bishop's crozier more was needed
Than pious converse. Denmark's Absalom
Has shown how well the steel cuirass can look
Over the soft white pallium—how the helmet
May fitly cover e'en a tonsured head;
That it becomes a bishop not to be
 Guileless alone, but full of strength and courage,

Like to a cherub clad in gleaming metal,
Guarding His Eden with wrath's mighty sword.
Yet by Augustine's wiles was Hakon taught
To seek himself a bishop, who should fill
His office—harmlessly.   I wish for thee
Prosperity in this thy lofty calling.

    Erland. I thank you, brother!   Let me walk in
        peace
My few remaining steps towards my grave !
I cannot stand much longer in your way.
Waste not the time !   This news concerning Axel
Grieves me far more.   Youth ever sees before him
The rising beams of hope : old age is used
To cold and storm.   The thoughtless boy
Has then forgotten——

    Knud.   Without doubt nor he
Nor Valborg knew it ; for as matters stood
Their mothers would be anxious to conceal
The circumstance.   The sturdy Thord Hunsfrei—
He was King Sigurd's man, as wild a warrior
As Sigurd here of Reine—now this Thord
Allowed his son, young Axel, for five years
To run about unchristened, like a heathen.

When Immer's daughter Valborg was baptized,
The Lady Helvig brought her to the font:
Thord prayed his kinswoman to take the boy,
So that he might no more be plagued about it.
And thus the children were baptized together,
Though Axel was the elder by five years.
In order to avoid all further scandal,
Their mothers hushed the tale. But in the book
Has John inscribed it. I was present
As famulus; and many witnesses
Are still alive who can confirm my words.

[*He shows him the entry in the church book.*

Erland. A fate most cruel follows Gille's race!

Knud. A fate most cruel always follows sin,
And strikes the sinner in the Gille race,
As in another. Now if Thord Hunsfreia
Had not delayed to let his son be christened,
Axel were not god-brother now to Valborg;
And loved not Axel, 'gainst the Church's canons,
His near relation, but some other maid,
No law would now impede his happiness.
Of all the Gille race is Hakon greatest;—
See! what is punishing the bold transgressor,

Will only crown with joy *his* virtuous life.

Erland. Alas! ye hapless ones!

Knud. I know full well
That such a circumstance, most reverend lord!
Must grieve your heart most sorely. You are old,
Your health, too, is not very good at present:
You think not well of Brother Knud, I know;
And yet he may have more devotion to you
Than you imagine. Go you now in peace
Back to the convent. I will make excuse
To Hakon for your absence, and I will
Perform the service for you willingly.

Erland. Perform the service willingly? Nay, nay
You shall not be their executioner.
It soothes the grief of the unfortunate
To hear the heavy doom of fate pronounced
Unwillingly by lips of kind compassion.
I will myself perform my cruel duty,
If it should cause mine aged heart to break.
With all my power I will strive to aid
The hapless pair. I will without delay
Write to the Pope to grant them dispensation
For this as for the other hindrance.

Knud.   Nay!
It is not to be thought of. Hadrian,
The Norseman's aged friend, is dead and gone.
Victor and Alexander now are fighting
About the popedom, and they seize all means
To gain the favour of each Christian prince.
King Hakon has acknowledged Alexander,
And Alexander then can hardly fail
To do a service in return to Hakon
In such a trifling matter.
   Erland.   " Trifling matter?"—
The happiness of two such noble hearts!
   Knud. So talks one in the pulpit certainly;
But in the Vatican and at the palace
State policy requires a different language.
   Erland. "State policy!" Ha, hell itself contains
No fouler monster in its gloomy pit,—
So it was Hydra fair, a Cerberus,
And Fenrir * in the heathenish Valhalla;
For they showed openly their ravenous jaws;
But this foul Satan, rich in every crime,
With boundless impudence will dare to call
His villany " sound sense," and hide the dagger

        * The monster wolf of Northern mythology.

Beneath a spotless robe, whilst he betrays
The innocent, like Judas, with a kiss.

  Knud. A glorious flow of words, most reverend father!

  Erland. Alas for him to whom the voice of truth
Is nought but words!

  Knud.   The bridal train draws near.

  Erland. Be strong, my aged heart, and drink thy
      cup!
Long has it been the duty of the priest
To follow hapless innocence unto
Its Golgotha.

  Knud.   Now must we to the choir,
That in procession we may issue thence
To meet the bridal train, and stay its course.

    [*During the singing of the chorale, the bridal train comes in the following order:—First, the royal guards with halberds; next a number of choir-boys in red kirtles and with caps of the same colour on their heads, carrying bridal-torches; Axel Thordson and Hakon; a number of knights two and two; a company of girls with baskets, from which they strew flowers on the church-floor; Queen Thora, who leads Valborg, clad in white satin, with a wreath of roses around her long hair; the queen's ladies and maidens two and two. The procession passes round Harald Gille's grave, and round both the pillars; and then it halts so that the men stand on the right side by Axel's, and the women on the left side by Valborg's family grave. The lovers kneel down and offer up a prayer beside their parents' tombs. In the background the royal guards arrange themselves in line, and before them stand the maidens and youths with flower-baskets and torches. In the midst, between the pillars, a view is given through the nave toward the high altar and the choir, whence the monks come in procession; Brother Knud with the church book, the Archbishop with his silver mounted crozier. Meanwhile the choir sings—*

"Whom God hath given a virtuous wife,
He owns the highest gift of life;
Full like a merchant-ship is she,
Bringing him great prosperity.

"Her tender hand oft plies the reel,
The distaff, and the spinning-wheel;
Rich carpets deck her husband's room,
All wrought upon her weaving-loom.

"In silken robes, as white as snow,
With purple fringes, doth she go;
While piety her lips express,
Within her heart dwells guilelessness.

"She gives her husband children too,
Her Fatherland Norwegians true.—
All joy and blessing you betide,
O happy youth! O happy bride!"

The Monks. "Gloria in Excelsis Deo!"

The Choir. "Amen!"

[*Axel and Valborg rise from prayer. King Hakon leads Axel to Valborg, the queen dowager Valborg to Axel. They give their hands to each other over Harald Gille's monument, and then turn in order to walk up hand-in-hand to the altar; amongst the pillars of the nave they are met by the choir of monks, when the archbishop stops them with his crozier.*

Erland. Unhappy ones ! the duty of his office
Obliges aged Erland here to stay
Your steps upon the flower-strewn path of hope.
Despair not of your fate ! Commit yourselves
Into the hands of God ; and do not hate
An aged man, whose highest joy had been
To bless your union, had the will of Heaven
Permitted him.

Axel. Great God !—O Christ ! what is it ?
Most reverend father ! have you not the bull ?
Have you not seen our marriage is allowed,
And that our tie of kinship is unloosed ?

Erland. My dearest son ! arm thee against thy fate
With hero-strength ! You may not marry Valborg.
Your kinship is indeed dissolved, but still
Ye are baptismal twins, brought to the font
At one and the same time, and by one woman :
Fru Helvig was godmother to you both.
Of this relationship the bull saith nought,
And such a marriage doth the Church forbid.

Axel. What sayest thou, bishop ? Gracious God !
My Valborg !
She swoons away. Help, maidens !

Valborg (supported by a maiden). Oh, 'tis nothing!
I was a little faint. Lend me thy shoulder,
Ivanhoide! It will quickly pass away.

   Axel. Baptismal twins?

   Knud (comes with the church book). Yes, yes! baptismal twins.

   Axel. Is 't written? Let me see, thou pale-faced Judas,
Thou liest, I hope. Nay, show it me; for Axel
Can also read. Show me——

   [*He gazes at the book, which Knud holds before him.*
                                  The letters run
Together when I look. [*He falls down at Valborg's feet.*
                      O Valborg! Valborg!
It is all o'er.

   Valborg.   Nay, nay!

   Axel (springs up).   It is all o'er!—
I see it plain,—see all that now must follow;
My striving through that weary five years' time,
To gain admission to the aged Pope,
To merit his esteem, and then his friendship,—
To let him know the secret of my heart;—
All was at length accomplished,—now it is

All lost and profitless.   If Hadrian lived,
What were it more than some few months' delay?
But he is dead; and Alexander lives—
A wily cardinal; and Hakon lives—
Mine enemy.   I see thee, wolf! thou glarest
Upon thy prey, and grinnest in thy wolf-shroud—
My staff is broke.   It is all o'er, my Valborg!
> [*He casts himself again on his knees, and hides his face in her hands.*

Erland (*with a stern look at the king*).   It was no good or pious act of thine,
To let this come to so extreme a point;
To keep two wretched hearts upon the strain
With short-lived hope, and at the latest hour
To let them see their hope's soap-bubble burst.
It was not right to shock the deepest feelings
Of one, whose sacred office, and whose age,
Alike demand respect, with this most sad,
Most pitiable sight.

Hakon.   The blame must fall
On Axel's Thordson's self: it was his rashness
That urged him hither to his speedy grief.
Had he but hearkened to his king's advice

He would have given time.   I cannot bar
The way to Church before my warriors' faces :
And 'tis through thee the Church's laws must speak.
> *Knud (comes with a linen cloth).* Since Axel Thord-
> son cannot marry Valborg,

The Church's laws require of them a token
Confirming their divorce.
> *Erland (to Hakon).* Surely, King Hakon,

We may omit the custom for this time !
> *Hakon.* My dignity requires that I should see

The laws fulfilled with strictness.   Do thy duty !
> *Erland (draws near the lovers).* My children !   O
> my children !   Seventy winters

Have crushed this aged heart : but never yet
A cup so bitter has it drunk.   My Axel !
Forgive an honest servant of the Lord
His duty !   'Tis not I,—'tis Fate that parts thee
From Valborg : but 'tis only a divorce
For this life ;—yonder may ye love for ever.
> *Axel* and *Valborg (kneel down before him, seize his
> hands, and kiss them).* O, my most reverend
> Father !

> *Erland.*   Dearest children !

Stand up, my Axel! Thou, sweet Valborg, too,
Stand up!—Lay hold upon this linen cloth,
My dearest friend! Take in your hand, poor maid,
This linen cloth.

> [*Axel and Valborg lay hold each of an end of the linen cloth. The king reaches his sword to the archbishop; he approaches to cut it asunder, but pauses.*

No, no! I cannot do it.—
Come, Brother Knud! a little while ago
You offered me your help. I am too old;
My hand is weak; I have forgotten how
To wield a sword these forty winters past.—
I cannot do it.

> *Knud.* Well, give me the sword;
> [*He draws near Axel and Valborg, steps between them with the sword in his hand, and says—*

The royal sword in spiritual hands
Here cuts in twain this linen cloth,—and so
Doth Heaven for ever part thee, Axel Thordson!
From Valborg, Immer's daughter.

> [*He cuts in sunder the cloth between them.*
> *The Monks* (*in the background*). Amen! Amen!

[*The maidens take off the red rose-wreath from Valborg's head, and a white one is placed instead.*

Hakon. Our work is done. Let them take Valborg now
Back to the convent. Pardon, noble mother!
If you have been eye-witness to a scene
That has offended you.

The Queen. May God forgive you!

Hakon (*reaches his hand to his mother, whilst he turns and looks at Axel and Valborg*). Our work is done. Let them be parted now!

Erland (*firmly*). Not yet! You sternly have insisted on
Fulfilment of a law, which could but pour
Its bitter wormwood on their sorrowing hearts.
Well, then, let me to your remembrance call
Another law, which generously allows
Such luckless ones, before they part, to take
Leave of each other.

Hakon (*waits*). Well, then, make it short!
Take leave, good Axel! of your sister Valborg.

Erland. Not thus was it intended: they have right
To speak to one another undisturbed.

Hakon. That foolishly occasion may be given
To light again the flame of sinful love.—
'Tis an unreasonable law.

Erland (*firmly*). But yet
A law it is that claims to be obeyed.

Hakon. And if the king should now abolish it?

Erland (*with dignity*). He would o'erstep the limit
of his power,—
I would pronounce him excommunicate.

Hakon. Ha,—you speak boldly.

Erland. Yes, as an archbishop.

Hakon. And who, then, made you an archbishop?

Erland. God.

Hakon. What sayest thou, old man?

Erland (*in a commanding tone, whilst he raises his crozier*). Let all depart!
Let these unhappy ones be granted time
To calm their troubled hearts, and bid farewell.

Hakon (*restrains himself*). True, you have right to
issue orders here.

[*He goes, with his followers. The archbishop gives a sign to Knud and the other monks, whereupon they retire to the choir.*

Erland. Nought shall intrude upon your silent grief.—
Ay, let your fainting hearts breathe freely now,
And bid your sad farewell before ye part.
The time that may be granted you is brief,—
Employ it, then. God strengthen you, poor children!
[*He goes.*

Axel. Thanks, thanks!—Thou coverest the thorn of grief
With pity's pallid rose.

Valborg (*takes the wreath off her hair, and gazes at it*). A token meet
Of sacred love these pure white roses are.
The earthly, ruddy blaze of Love is quenched.
These snow-white leaves are spread like angels' wings.

Axel. O Valborg!

Valborg. Nay, take comfort, dear-loved friend!

Axel. What! I take comfort?—and say, how canst thou
So readily compose thyself?

Valborg. I was
Prepared for this.

Axel. "Prepared?" Nay, Valborg! nay

A little while ago I saw thy joy.
How sweetly smiled thy lip, my darling girl!
How thine eye glistened!

 Valborg.   Ay, the eye will glisten
With brightest lustre, when 'tis full of tears.

 Axel. Could Valborg doubt? For did not all betoken
Our happiness? And have I like a fool
Rushed madly towards a visionary joy?
Like Jacob, have I not with ceaseless toil
Worked year by year, with steadfast aim to earn
My Rachel?—Must not then a blow like this
Now crush my very heart? No, no! my fate
Could ne'er have been foreseen, and now it breaks
My spirit quite.—Ay, you were right, my Valborg!
When you beheld the pilgrim kneeling yonder,
He was beside his grave, and not his goal.
Ay, you were right! it opens its embrace—
A faithful friend's embrace. What have I now
To seek for longer in the wide, wide world?
My sun is set, my light of life is quenched.
Come, open thou my grave! Thou,—thou art warm:

Come, open thou, and clasp me to thy breast!
My Valborg dares not clasp me now to hers.
    Valborg. Yes, Axel, yes! Though 'tis for the last time,
Valborg dare clasp thee to her heart once more.
    Axel. O Fate! come strike me dead within these arms!
    Valborg. No, Axel! speak not thus. No, you must live!
    Axel. What should I live for?
    Valborg.   Live for honour, Axel!
Do not forget your glorious hero-name :—
"Great," "noble," "rich," doth "Axel" signify
In Norway's ancient tongue.
    Axel.   Ay, that had Axel,—
Ay, that had Axel been, if cruel fate
Had not thus robbed him of Valhalla's joy,
His hero-meed, his Valborg.
    Valborg.   Dear-loved youth!
    Axel. The trumpet called me to the din of battle,
But not to win a fading oak-leaf crown :
I saw thee, as my Norna, on the cloud;

Thy hand held forth to me a wreath of roses,—
Of bright red roses.

    Valborg.   Ah! 'tis withered now.

    Axel. I went to Rome; I saw the aged Pope:
With trembling knees I bowed before his throne:
But from his father-smile, I drank fresh life,
Whilst in my hand he placed the magic brief.
Ye snow-clad mountains of fair Italy,
How quickly sank ye in the far horizon!
Mine eye, intently gazing on the North,
Already seemed to see the northern lights,
Gleaming like memories of its distant home.

    Valborg. It was thy Valborg's feelings, O my Axel!

    Axel. Unwearied went the youthful pilgrim on,
Now over mountains, now through valleys low,
Far from his hearth, his pilgrim-staff in hand.
A hope assured of coming happiness
Lightened his longing, soothed his home-sick heart.
The lark's song wakened him, and sang of Valborg,
The morning red beamed brightly as his love.
The mid-day drove him to the shady wood;
On many a southern stem, on German beeches,
Stands Valborg's name.   Oh hasten, wrinkled bark!

To hide from sight those letters dear.   O Dryad!
Sing in the stem with soft and plaintive voice
Of that unhappy pair in northern lands,
For southern shepherdesses, whilst thou wavest
Thy leafy tresses in the evening wind.

   Valborg. O Axel! Axel! hast thou loved me so?

   Axel. Now shalt thou see me yet again, O world!
But without pilgrim-staff,—my staff is broke.
Now shall I wander through the trees once more—
Through forest dark—but without aim or object.
The first low knoll upon my lonely path
Can give me all I seek for now—a grave:
There is my home.

   Valborg.   O cruel one! and wilt thou
Forsake thy Valborg?

   Axel.   And should Axel stay
To see thee dragged by Hakon as his victim
To yonder altar?

   Valborg..   Sooner shall he drag me
To public execution!

   Axel.   Savage tiger!
A heart like this thou crushest—and yet darest
To call it love?

Valborg.   Mine eye, bedimmed with tears,
Will not be able long to bear the light :
Before Death closes it, my mother kind,
The Holy Church, will lend to me her veil.
    Axel. O God! my Valborg be a nun? This hair—
These long, gold, silken tresses—must they be
Shorn off? this form of loveliness enshrouded
In coarse, stiff, hideous, garments black?
    Valborg.   And then
Here shall I wander many a night alone,
And think upon my darling dream, and on
Thy coming home, and on our cruel fate.
Then shall my heart lift up itself to God
In prayer and holy song; and for the sake
Of Valborg's prayer the Lord will comfort thee.
    Axel. O Valborg!
    Valborg.   And within my little cell
I shall sit silent, broidering gold in silk,
And quietly live on my mournful life;
Like to the turtle-dove, that ne'er finds peace
With all her piety,—that never rests
On leafy spray, aweary though she be,—

That never drinks from out the fountain clear,
Ere she has muddied it with restless feet.

Axel. And Axel?

Valborg. Go thou straightway to thy home,
Up to thy sister, to the gentle Helfred.
Do not in madness leave thy Fatherland,
Nor linger on a spot where, day by day,
Thy wrathful mood would gain upon thee.—Time
Heals everything, and it will heal thy wound.
Great Nature, in her silent majesty,
A gentle sister's love, will soothe thy grief
More than the merriest company. Go then
From hence unto thy home, which towers aloft
Upon the mountain brow, and proud looks down
Over the valley and the wild sea-waves;
And thus shalt thou look down upon thy fate.
And when thy heart begins to beat too strong,
Then take thy spear, thy bow, and cast thyself
Into the dark pine-forest; spend thy rage
Upon the bear, and on the savage lynx,
That vex the forest's peace. And in this wise
Thou by degrees may'st overcome thy grief.
On winter evenings shalt thou sit beside

Thy sister Helfred in the raftered hall,
And read aloud to her from ancient Sagas
Of Odin, Thor, and of the gentle Baldur.
To Helfred's harp thou mayest also sing,—
But guard thee well 'gainst Signe's, Hagbarth's lay,
Nor sing thou e'er of Aag and Jomfrue Else.
[*She bursts into tears.*

Axel. O Valborg! Valborg! these shall be my lays. [*He embraces her.*

Erland (*returns*). My children! now 'tis time—it must be so :
Relentless fate compels me ;—ye must part !

Valborg. Farewell !

Axel. Farewell !

Valborg. We meet again.

Axel. With God

[*They tear themselves from one another's arms, and go each to his side, Valborg with her attendants. One becomes aware of Wilhelm in the background.*

Erland. Noble, yet luckless children ! Like a star
Your light of love its pale reflection casts
Upon my memory's wintry sky. Ah, yes,—

'Tis an unhealthy heart that never felt
The power of love. Thou knowest not, good
    Axel!
That Erland's fate was very like to thine.—
Eleonora!—Like the moonlight, beams
Thy memory down on my December snow.
Oh wert thou true to me till death? No lips—
No lips have ever brought thine Erland tidings
Of thee, and of thy fate.

    Wilhelm (*in the background*). Eleonora
Of Hildesheim was true to thee till death.

    Erland. Is it a voice from out the grave that
    speaks?

    [*He turns round, and becomes aware of Wilhelm.*

    Wilhelm. Forced by her father Gebhard's cruel
    will
To marry Rudolf, was Eleonora
To Erland true at heart: and thee she loved
In thought, whilst, prisoned in the gloomy castle,
Her mournful life was spent with one she hated.

    Erland. Who can yon stranger be, so pale and
    wan,
Who answers thus the thought of my sad heart?

Is it a revelation? There he stands,
Still as a statue, leaning on his sword.
                      [*Wilhelm goes towards him.*
  Erland. Who art thou, foreigner?
  Wilhelm.   A cross between
The lamb and tiger, my most reverend father!
A snow-flower brought up in the cold, beneath
A horoscope most strange,—the planet Venus
Was by a fiery comet then eclipsed.
  Erland. Thou art——
  Wilhelm.   A son of thine Eleonora—
Of thy deadly foeman, Rudolf.
  Erland.   All ye saints!
Thou!—can it be? Ah yes! I know them now,
Those features dear; I see them mingled with
The frigid sternness. O my son! my son!
Eleonora's son, come to my arms,—
Come, let me clasp thee to my aged heart!
  Wilhelm. I feel it all as true and warm as thou,
But Nature has denied me tears, my father!
  Erland. What is thy name, Eleonora's son?
  Wilhelm. "Wilhelm;" or, in your Northern speech,
      "Vildhjálmur."

Erland. What angel then has brought thee here to
    me?

Wilhelm. One of the good, I hope, most reverend
    lord.

Most strange my nature is, and half a monster;
Made up of most conflicting elements,—
Of love and hate, of scorn and tenderness.
I feel within my breast a ceaseless longing,
Which only finds relief when I can plunge
Into the thickest of the fight,—or when,
With mute and cold, but steadfast faithfulness,
I join me to an honourable friend :—
So have I joined me now to Axel Thordson.
I cannot love myself; but yet I find
Solace in giving aid to one who loves.
I came with him. I knew that you were here :
My mother had, upon her bed of death,
Charged me most solemnly to visit you.
She knew that you had changed the coat of mail
For canon's hood, and earnestly she prayed me
Some day to bear to you her life's farewell.
Forgive ! 'mid war's alarms I had forgotten it
For full ten years. At last young Axel's journey

Called back to mind my promise, and awakened
My conscience. I believe my heavy mood
Has been a punishment, which now will vanish
When I have done my mother's dying will.
Most reverend father, lay on this wild head
Your sacred hand, and give to me your blessing.
                              [*He kneels down.*

  Erland. God bless thee!
  Wilhelm.   Thanks! it is already lighter.
                              [*He rises.*
I see the hand of Heaven in this our meeting.—
See, venerable sir, you lost your bride
Long years ago, and Wilhelm's heart as well
Is closed 'gainst love. But here there are two hearts,
Each made to love the other, whom they part.
Well then, most reverend father! let us two,—
The one the victim, and the other fruit,
Of an unholy union,—hinder now
Its repetition, and so save our friends.

  Erland. My son, how can we?
  Wilhelm.   That depends on you;
But I can save them.
  Erland.   How, my dearest son?

Wilhelm. Our ship is lying ready in the fjord,
And can set sail soon as the anchor's weighed.
Valborg was taken to the convent : thither
The only way lies through the church. To hinder
Her carrying off,—which Hakon well might fear,—
Shall Friar Knud, with twenty knights in arms,
Himself keep watch to-night by the church door,
And give th' alarm upon the slightest noise.

   Erland. And can such watchfulness, which makes a
      rescue
Impossible, delight you?

   Wilhelm.   Watchfulness
Of such a kind alone makes rescue possible ;
For were the thick and iron-bound church-door
Closed, there could be no rescue ; and to-morrow
Would Hakon carry Valborg home a bride.
But through their twenty knights in arms, and through
  Yon scowling monk, the one-and-twentieth,
I can well make my way.

   Erland.   But will the skirmish
Not give alarm, and wake the castle guards?

   Wilhelm. The holy church floor shall nowise be
      stained

With honourable blood of valiant men,
Obeying duty and their king's command :
I know a better means.

 Erland.   And what, my son ?

 Wilhelm. Is not yon golden chest above the altar
Saint Olaf's shrine ? And is it not believed
That many a time, upon occasion given,
Saint Olaf's body rises from his tomb
At midnight, as a ghost, to terrify
Transgressors, and to comfort and support
Oppressèd virtue ?

 Erland.   So do all believe.

 Wilhelm. Have you not, as archbishop, his gold
   helmet,
His iron-pointed spear, and silver-spangled robe,
Under your charge ?

 Erland.   Yes.

 Wilhelm.   Then is Axel saved !

 Erland. My friend, you would——

 Wilhelm.   And do you hesitate
Whether the old tradition may for once
Be suffered to assist a righteous cause,
As oft misused it has promoted wrong ?

Erland. No, no! it is no sin.   God will forgive
The honest-minded, innocent deceit
Which utmost need demands for virtue's rescue.
   Wilhelm. "Deceit!" and who has said it is deceit?
Saint Olaf comes himself, most reverend father!—
Himself he comes,—he clothes himself in me:
I am his spectre.   Is a spectre not
The earthly shroud of an immortal spirit?
   Erland. It cannot well be otherwise defined.
   Wilhelm. Well then, I am Saint Olaf's pallid shroud.
'Tis he has put this thought into my soul;
And so as Olaf's real ghost I come.
   Erland. My son, with what strange fire thine eye is gleaming!
   Wilhelm. My thoughts dwell chiefly in eternity;
And many a time ere now the spirit-world
Has stood revealed before my trancèd sight.—
I went on bóard the ship, where sundry things
Had to be set in order.   On the deck
The sun beat fiercely.   Then, my business done,
I hastened to the church, so that I might
Be present at the marriage.   Came too soon.

And then, so cool and silent was the place,
That wearied with my work,—when many times
Through nave and aisles and chapels I had wandered,—
Observed each holy altar, spelt the names
On many a tombstone,—I sat down at last,
Leaning against a pillar of the choir,
Where, green with age, the copper harness hangs,
And where full many a soiled and dusty shred
Of ancient martial banners floats above.
Over against Saint Olaf's golden shrine
I fell asleep. Unquiet was my dream,
And sorrowful; for what was taking place
I also saw, as through transparent mist.
And when the monk foul-minded cut in twain
The cloth, I sprang up in a rage, to haste
To Axel's aid. But straightway terrified,
Down sank I to the ground again; for, as
The cloth was parted, yonder saintly shrine
Yawned open, and within the coffin rose
A wrathful form, and gazed upon the monk.

Erland. And how appeared he?

Wilhelm.   Like a warrior strong,
Of middle stature, with light golden hair,

And deep blue eyes; a blood-stained cloth he held
In his left hand, and pressed it to his wound.

   Erland. Ah! that was Olaf's ghost.

   Wilhelm.   He pointed up
Towards the armour hanging over me,
And cried, " Thou shalt to-night in Olaf's armour
Punish foul treachery, and true love defend:
Undimmed its sacred light shall ever burn!"—
He said, and vanished. And as I awaked,
I heard at the church door the King's loud voice
Issue his cruel order to the monk.

   Erland. Follow me, chosen Wilhelm! I am
      ready.

   Wilhelm. The time is not yet come.—When day-
      light dies,
And cold the dew is falling on the graves,
And doubt upon the courage of the bold,
And fear upon the sinner's conscience; when
The church is full of deep mysterious darkness,
And through the gloom a faint and flickering ray
Falls from the altar-lamp upon the tombs;—
When its twelfth stroke the deep-toned bell hath
      tolled;

When hoots the midnight owl, and crows the cock,—
Then rises Olaf in his kingly pride,
As king of night, to punish villainy,
To fell the villain, and to wipe the tears
From off the eyes of injured innocence.

ACT IV.

ACT IV.

NIGHT. *The lamp burns feebly in the twilight. Friar* KNUD *is sitting with* BJÖRN, GAMLE, KOLBEIN, *and several warriors, on a bench beside right-hand pillar in the church.*

Knud. Here were it best to sit, my worthy friends;
Beside this pillar, by the holy crosses
Of our three great and blessed Northern Kings.
Here let us then, in God's name, pass the night.
Endrid! have you kept watchful eye upon
Those soldiers at the door?

Endrid (comes). Yes; they keep guard.

Knud. Well, we will also keep our guard. A subject
Ought to be watchful of his sovereign's safety:
And therefore have I chosen out this spot,

By the " King's pillar," as they call it: sacred
It rises o'er us with its crosses three.
But see the other pillar opposite !
" Pillar of Shame " it should be called in future.
There had the two enamoured sinful ones
Graven their names. They foolishly defied
Both royal power and Holy Church's law.
Now comes the punishment of God, of justice !
In noble wrath the King has with his sword
Cut down this cipher, which profanely dared
To spot the Church's wood with lovers' garlands ;
And now their garland withers in the dust.

 Björn. Aye, aye !—and what are flowers fit for else
Than so to wither ? Let the garland lie !
With the King's cross 'tis very different.
The loftier it is, the safer stands
The lands' condition, and the higher rises
The realm in might and honour. Therefore like I
The uppermost among these crosses three
The best of all. The other two, indeed,
Are pretty high ; but they do not approach
The lofty Harald.

Knud. Speak not so, good friend.
Olaf, of blessed memory, stands no whit
Below King Harald Haarderaade : peace
Has never flourished more than under him ;
And he was, too, the clergy's surest stay.
    Björn. There was the mischief! Understand me
       rightly :
I mean the peace,—the clergy, reverend sir,
Is worthy of all honour, I well know.
But Olaf Kyrre, Magnus Barfod, laid
The germs of Norway's weakness and destruction,
By altering the nation's ancient customs.
And therefore think I they do not come nigh
That glorious hero, Harald Haarderaade.
    Knud. Our land has profited by Olaf's deeds.
    Björn. Ere Olaf Kyrre's time men drank from
       horns,
The fire burned on mid-floor in the hall,
And Norway's king sat midmost of his men
Upon his long bench, while the ale was served him
Across the hearth. This did not suit King Olaf:
He needs must have a high seat reared for him
Upon the dais-bench. In the hall no longer

The fire was left to burn with merry blaze;
It must be stowed into a hole, aside,
But for this reason, that their weakly lungs
Could not endure the smoke.
 Knud.   Well, father Björn,
It falls upon the chest.
 Björn.   Pooh! chest, indeed;
An honest fellow must have in his chest
Courage, and never mind a fume or smoke.
But speaking of the dress,—there surely has
King Olaf heavy sins; and may the Lord
Forgive him for them in his grave! Before,
The warrior in his armour used to go,
Or in white wadmel kirtle; now, his breeches
Were laced around his loins with gold and silver,
Gold rings his legs encircled, and in folds
Soft silk was laid upon his arms and shoulders,—
Although the sleeve itself was made so tight
An instrument was used to draw it on.
With Magnus Barfod it was full as bad,
Though in a different way. He was a hero;
But, after his campaign in Ireland, ran he,
With cut-short kirtle and with naked legs,

Not through the streets, like any beggar, though
He was the King of Norway? Has he not
Himself to thank for getting such a nickname?

 Knud. Well, father, all things change with time,
  we know.

 Björn (*shakes his head*). Had they but had the
  grace to hold in honour
The ancient drinking-horn, the rest might pass;
But to sip ale and mead out of a cup,
That is a fashion which will bring the land
Sooner or later to complete destruction.
A courteous knight would always drain his measure,
And not set down beard-drippings on the table.

 Endrid. Well, there old Björn is right: King Harald
  was
A noble hero. In the Grecian land
The name of Harald stands in high renown,
E'en from the days when with Varangian hosts
He served Queen Zoe.

 Björn.   Endrid, you come straight
From Micklegarth:* how goes it? Are ye still
Honour to th' ancient North, as in my young days?

 * *i. e.*, Constantinople, so called by the Northern Varangians.

Endrid. All has not quite died out with you, good
    fellow.

Björn. Ye sleep then still upon the hard, bare ground,
With helmet on your head, with shield on breast,
With sword above your head, with your right hand
Upon the hilt,—with courage in your heart?

Endrid. No otherwise.

Björn.   And rides King Olaf still,
The saintly spectre, on his snow-white steed
Ahead of you, when 'gainst the foe ye march?

Endrid. It happens oft, good father Björn. Have you
Not heard the story of what lately happened
With Neiter,—with his sword?

Björn.   No, son; relate it.

Endrid. You know that Ingebjörn, a gallant Swede,
Seized on this sword that time King Olaf fell
At Stiklestad. 'Twas handed down from him
To son and grandson, and his last descendant
Shared with me in the last imperial war.
Our tents were struck: the Vœrings lay asleep,
Just as you say, each in his armour, with
His sword in his right hand, above his head.
But when the Swede awakes, he has no sword;

It lies flung far from him upon the field.
So went it with him three successive nights :
Then asked the emperor what this could mean ?
"Ah!" answered he, " my noble Kyrialax "—
(Which signifies, " My Lord Alexius,"—
For " Kyrie " in Greek is "Lord," you know,—
The Prayer-book tells us)—" Kyrialax," he said,
" This sword which I possess, its name is ' Neiter ; '—
Twas Olaf's sword, which with his life he lost
At Stiklestad."

 Björn. A deed well done, by King Olaf!
To wrest the sword out of the Swede's right hand.
What right had he to own King Olaf's sword?

 Endrid. Aye, aye ! that saw the emperor and all.
Then Kyrialax had, at a vast expense,
A church built for St Olaf, on the spot
Where lay his sword, and there above the altar
The sword itself was hung,—just as his coffin
Stands here above the altar in the choir.

 Kolbein. How weirdly from the gilded royal shrine
The light is gleaming towards us through the gloom !
But is it true, my reverend father, walks
King Olaf here at midnight ?

Björn.   'Tis a question!

Knud. Ye Norsemen are a most unruly folk;
And so it is found needful, that at times
The very dead should rise from out their graves,
To call you to repentance and amendment.

Björn. Have you ne'er heard the hundred miracles?

Kolbein. Aye, that I have: but then I hardly know
Whether I should believe them.

Knud.   Don't blaspheme,
Son! you might doubt as well of Heaven itself,
And of your own salvation, as of Olaf,
And of his miracles.

Björn.   Kolbein! take care
It fare with you not as with the Danish earl
Who lost his eyesight for his unbelief.

Endrid. Björn! tell us somewhat of the holy saint.
Your years, we know, have seen full many a marvel.

Kolbein. Nay, it will but excite imagination;
And since we have to keep our guard to-night
Within the church——

Björn.   Are you a coward?

Kolbein.   Nay!
Not for the living.

Björn.   Answered well, my son!
Have you a conscience clear?
   Kolbein.   Yea, that have I.
   Björn.   Well,—
You need not be afraid then of the dead.
King Olaf will not injure any here;
For all of us,—if I except alone
The pious Knud,—have heavy sins;
Yet is our conscience clear; and consequently
Saint Olaf will not do us any harm.
   Endrid. Relate!
   Björn.   It was one midnight here in Kjöping,
Just as the clock struck twelve——
                           [*The clock strikes twelve.*
   Endrid.   Ha,—did you hear?
   Björn. I am not deaf!—Just as the clock struck twelve,
And when the cock had crowed his midnight crow——   [*The cock crows.*
   Kolbein. Hearken! it crows!
   Björn (*provoked*).   If I shall tell my tale,
Then you must hold your tongue. What nonsense this!

One can no longer hear one's own voice speak,
For all these clocks that strike, and cocks that
  crow,
And fools that chatter. 'Tis an ugly habit,
When youths impertinently interrupt
The story :—in my day the youths were silent
Whene'er an aged warrior spoke. But where
Did we leave off?

 Endrid.   At cock-crow.

 Björn.   True.—(*To Kolbein*)—If you
Break in upon my story, you may ask
A toothless crone to tell you all the rest.—
Well, then, one midnight here at twelve o'clock,
Just when the cock had crowed, Saint Olaf came
Slowly from out the choir, and down the nave,
In golden armour, with his vizor closed,
And on his helmet the carbuncle crown,
With his long spear and silver-spangled robe,
Whose train swept after him the temple floor.

  [*A form appears in the background of the church,
    just similar to that described by Björn.
    Kolbein, who first becomes aware of it,
    turns pale, and gazes fixedly towards it.*

What is the matter with you, silly boy?
　　　　　　　　　　[*Kolbein is silent.*
Well, Kolbein! Have you lost your tongue, I
　　pray!

Kolbein. If you narrate, I must not interrupt
Your story. Only I may venture now
To mention by the way, that yonder stands
A man, precisely such as you describe.

　The Soldiers. Christ save us! 'Tis the ghost!
　　[*The monk flies:—some are about to follow
　　him.*

Björn.　　　　　　　Stay! are ye Norsemen?
Stay! are ye honourable, faithful soldiers?
He is a coward, and an evil-doer
Who flees. Kneel down upon your knees,
As I. See, thus! And now make bare your heads,
And reverently fold your hands. Ay, thus!
He is a common thief, who flees affrighted
From Olaf's ghost. Of what are ye afraid?
He is our patron saint. Why would ye flee?
Perchance he comes to speak to us his children.

　Kolbein. It draws still nigher.

　The Soldiers.　　　　Oh, may God protect us!

The Ghost (*in a deep voice*).
    Who dares in midnight darkness
        To break my death-sleep?
    Who calls the king at cock-crow
        From out his coffin?
    What sounds profane the silence
        Of Olaf's slumbers?
    Now, linger not, but leave ye,
        With swords and lances,
    In haste this dwelling holy
        Of saints and heroes!
    No word must any whisper
        Of what ye witness,
    Ere golden sunlight gildeth
        My shrine with glory.

[*The Soldiers rise up, bow, cross themselves, and leave the church.*

Knud (*comes back with the guard of the door*). I tell you it is nothing but imposture!
It was but my surprise which thus at first
Made it a little strange ere I could think.
There stands he: now come on! We are enough.
Take up your station round him with your halberds,

And capture him alive for me, the juggler!
Ghosts never haunt,—'tis only superstition.
They would deceive the king: but overcome
Your foolish fears! Saint Olaf is but dust,—
A bag of worms: his power is past and gone.

> [*The form rushes with hasty steps upon Knud,
> and thrusts the spear through his breast.*

The Soldiers. Christ save us! He is fallen in his
sin!
Fly, fly! Praise be to God and all His saints!

> [*They all fly, and the spectre vanishes.*

Knud (*alone*). It is my death-wound. Help! Oh,
save me! Help!
Forsake me not in mine extremity!
Ah,—I am left alone; I bleed to death.
Was it a human being? But he struck
His spear in me with an unnatural strength,
Right through the breast-plate, which my cloak concealed.
No, no! it was a mortal. All is mortal:
I know that there is no eternity.

> [*The clock strikes a quarter-past one.*

Ha,—what denotes that deep and solemn knell:

Th' eternal voice,—the unison on high?
O fear! O cruel, icy-cold despair!—
Is nothing near, wherewith to stanch the blood?

[*He feels about, and finds Valborg's wreath, which Hakon had cut down.*

Here—here are herbs wherewith to stanch the blood.
It flows still faster! What is this? O God!
It is fair Valborg's wreath of flowers. Mercy,—
Compassion! Pray, oh pray to God for me,
Ye youthful lovers! See my heart's red blood
Has stained your wreath! Oh pray, oh pray for me!

[*He dies.*

[*Wilhelm returns with Valborg and the archbishop.*

Wilhelm. Tremble not, noble maiden! you are saved.
My page is speedy, and he fetches Axel;
The wind is good, and all is clear on board,
And Fortune's elves already swell for us
The good ship's sails; fair Freia's beaming star
Twinkles adown from the dark vault of night.

Erland. My son! God bless thee for this deed of thine!

Wilhelm. My deed is trifling, father Erland. Thee
Must Axel thank for this his happiness.

Valborg. Ah, Wilhelm! both of you we both must
thank.

Wilhelm. Where is he?

Axel (*comes with sword and shield*). Wilhelm!
dearest Valborg! Father!

Wilhelm. Is the way open to the ship, good
Axel?

Axel. The street is clear. I saw the coward crew
Rush forth from the church-door, as though it were
A swarm of flies which one was chasing out
With linden twigs. The monk alone was wanting:
He should be seized forthwith, and put in chains.
I fear, if he is hidden in a corner,
That he may still betray us.

Wilhelm. Do not fear!
Foul treachery has reached its barrier.

[*He shows him the monk's corpse.*

Axel. Knud in his blood!

Valborg. O holy Virgin!

Erland (*with a terrified look at Wilhelm*).
Murdered?

H

Wilhelm (calmly). Nay,—slain. His rashness and his unbelief
Have driven the scoffer on the ice-cold spear
Of Fate, and of Saint Olaf.
  Erland.   Poor, blind sinner!
Gone hence impenitent and unabsolved.
  Axel. But see! what holds he in his pale, clenched hands?
My Valborg's wreath! Close to his heart he pressed it
In his death agony.
  Valborg.   Poor, wretched man!
Remorse had smitten him. God pardon him!
  Axel. That will He for thy prayer, thou noble girl!—
O joy! mine eyes once more behold my Valborg?
  Valborg. Two angels have delivered us from death.
  Wilhelm. Two mortal men! And now, my loving pair,
Now all depends on haste. The danger past,
And when the lofty Schwarzburg, with its wall,
And its strong tower, securely shelters us;
When Father Erland in the castle chapel—

Where Leonore was forced to marry Rudolph—
Shall join your hands together, then will be
Full time for your caresses. Then shall ye
Transform our Schwarzburg to a Weissenfels;
Then shall our Father Erland see himself
Grow young in you,—rude Wilhelm meek and mild;
And then may we sing masses for the peace
Of this poor sinner's soul. But now, my friends!
Pray cut the matter short, and follow Wilhelm.

Valborg. Christ! how my heart is beating!

Axel. Let us kneel
At Harald's grave, and bid our Fatherland
A last farewell!

> [*Whilst the lovers are kneeling, three hollow-
> sounding notes of a horn are heard afar off.*

Wilhelm. What now? Who is 't approaches?—
Fear not, my noble maiden! It is Gotfred,
My honourable, faithful page.—What news,
My Gotfred? What can mean those trumpet-notes?

Axel. I know them well: it was a battle-trumpet.

Gotfred. All aids our flight. Within this very hour
Has Erling Skakke run into the fjord
From Bergen with a numerous fleet, in order

To fall upon King Hakon Herdebred.
The horn ye heard sounded from Erling's ship,
As signal of attack. Nought hinders now
Our instant flight, for all is in confusion.

Wilhelm. The wrathful Norna goes with hasty steps
Towards her revenge. Come on, my gallant brother!
That thou shouldst draw thy sword against thy kinsman,
I know full well thy noble soul forbids.
Well, then, thou mayest leave him to his fate.—
But follow, where thy favouring Norna beckons.

Axel. (*after a moment's silence.*) My favouring
Norna beckons me to duty.

Wilhelm. What? Thinkest thou——

Axel. That now I cannot sail:
It is impossible,—impossible!

Wilhelm. Thou wilt——

Axel. Defend King Hakon Herdebred.

Wilhelm. Your enemy?

Axel. What enemy?—on him
I lately turned my back in scorn:—my king
Is now in need,—to him I owe my life.

Wilhelm. Axel! you owe your life to Fatherland,—

Not Hakon. Think you to advantage Norway
By fighting for his cause,—the mad young fool,
Who tramples under foot all duty for
His passion—who despises woman's virtue,
His subjects' sacred rights—who quite forgets
The public welfare for his private ends?—
No, Axel! no! Whoever would be king,
King-like he ought to think and act. Come;—
    Erling
Is a renowned, and brave, and noble chieftain.
Hinder not then his victory: he will not
Misuse it. Let old Norway's sceptre glisten
In hero-hands;—it rusts in those of cowards.

    Axel. Let not your lips with specious subtlety,
Pervert the honest judgment of your heart.
King Hakon is no coward:—monkish craft
Found out the way to play upon his passion.
Crossed love, ungoverned youth, and evil counsel,—
One of the three was quite enough to spoil
The best of hearts. He tries with haughty hand
To rob me of my bride: I would not bear it.
Another now would rob him of his kingdom:
As little will I suffer this. He is

My kinsman : Erling speaks insultingly
Of our forefather Harald : he would humble—
Uproot the Gille race, so that he might
Set his own son upon the throne of Norway.
Were I a Throndhjemer of Gille blood,
If I should suffer this ?—a man of honour,
If I should fail King Hakon in his need?
Have I not laid my hand in Hakon's hand?
Would Axel still deserve this lily-wand,
Thy friendship, being faithless to his king?

 Erland. Heroic youth ! you speak the words of
  duty.
Haste thee to draw thy sword, and save thy king,
Oh, would to God mine aged limbs had strength
To follow thee !

 Wilhelm. Cheer thou the lonely maid,
And I will fill thy place in battle, father !
I do not know the state of things so well
As thou and Axel. If ye both believe
That loyal duty calls him to the fight,—
Well, then, my sword is drawn,—I follow him.

 Axel. Oh weep not, Valborg ! all my fear is
  past ;

My heart is beating heavily no longer.
I will not steal my Valborg,—nay, but I
Will win her. Oh, our great forefather Harald!
Now first I understand thee. On thy sword
Thou lay'st thine hand, and say'st, "Defend mine
    honour!
Leave not thy Fatherland!"—Well, my beloved!
Let us propitiate a hostile fate,
And Hakon's self. The thoughtless youth shall learn
In war the value of an honest fighter;
And he himself, after the victory won,
Shall join thy hand, my Valborg, to thy wooer's,
Here, on his grave who now shall be avenged.

                    [*The trumpet sounds.*

Hildur!* I come. Thy warriors come to make thee
An offering of blood in Throndhjem's fjord.
Look, my beloved one! two hearts united
Stand blazoned glowing red on Axel's shield,
Part on the azure, part on argent ground.
That signifies, "Love, Innocence, and Heaven."
Valborg! our love is innocent, and Heaven
Will soon reward it.

      .   * Goddess of War.

Valborg. With eternal bliss.

Axel. In my great haste I have forgot to buckle
My scabbard on; I only seized the sword.

Valborg (takes a blue scarf from her shoulder).
Come, dear-loved warrior! let me bind on thee
Thy shoulder scarf!

*Axel. (kneels down: Valborg hangs the scarf over
his shoulder.)* O my most precious Valborg!
I am thy knight; how canst thou have a doubt
Of victory?

Valborg. Thou art my warrior; and I
Am thy Valkyria.*

Axel. Oh, weep not, Valborg!

Valborg. Nay, I will weep no longer. Woman,
Axel!
Can also show her courage by endurance.
Go then, my chosen friend, my darling hero!
Thy Valborg gives thee to our Fatherland.

Wilhelm. A noble maiden,—by St Innocence!
Farewell, most reverend father!

Erland. Oh, my sons!
God's angels follow and protect you both.

* Goddess of Fight.

Axel. Farewell, my Valborg!

Valborg (*holds him back in her arms*). Stay a
    moment yet!
Let me once more again, for the last time,
Gaze on my Axel's glorious hero-eye.

Axel (*kisses her*). Farewell!

Valborg. Go now! I never can forget thee.

                                      [*They part.*

ACT V.

ACT V.

Axel *enters with* King Hakon, *who is wounded in the right arm.*

Axel. Here are we safe awhile, my lord and king!
Here in God's holy house. Come, sit you down,
And let me bind for you your wounded arm;—
A warrior ought to know the art of healing;
One has not always help at hand. The wound
Is deep, but yet not dangerous. Now, had we
A piece of linen only!

Hakon.   This your kindness
Wounds me more deep than Erling Skakke's sword.

Axel. Be thou not wounded by my faithfulness,
Far other was its purpose.

[*He feels in his bosom, draws out a cloth, and starts,
but instantly composes himself, and says—*

                              Here is linen.

Hakon. Axel! why startest thou? Almighty God!
I know that cloth too well.

Axel. Nay, calm yourself.

Hakon. And with this cloth you wish to bind my
   arm?

Axel. So that you may not die from loss of blood.

Hakon. You wish to bind it with this very cloth
Wherewith I rent your life in twain?

Axel. My lord!
It is another cloth.

Hakon. Nay, nay! It is
The very cloth which that malicious Knud
Cut with my sword 'twixt you and Valborg, Axel!
I know it. Oh, swathe not my arm with this;
It burns me—tortures me with double pain.

Axel. Nay, it is natural a wound should burn,
And bandaging a sore is always painful.
Be calm, and rest yourself a moment, king!
Then in your left hand take your sword, and come
Once more with Axel 'gainst your haughty foe—
The presence of their king supports his people—
And I will serve instead of your right hand.

Hakon. Is it contempt, a lurking, proud revenge?

Or is it natural high-mindedness?
How shall I understand you, Axel? Think you
To heap up coals of fire on Hakon's head?

Axel. By God and man! I will be true to you;
I will not harm you; I will ne'er forsake you.

Hakon. This generosity but hurts me more.
O most unhappy Hakon Herdebred!
Thy bravest warrior despises thee.

Axel. By God in heaven, and by my Valborg,
    Hakon!
I do respect you.

Hakon.   I believe you, kinsman;
That was a solemn oath—well,—is it so;—
For Hakon acted like an ardent lover
Upon the throne—not like a coward, Axel!

Axel. Who feels the power of love and does not
    know
Its mighty workings?

Hakon.   Now your words are drawn
Out of my very heart, my gallant hero;
Your faithfulness and kindness move me so.

                  [*With sudden wildness.*

And yet, did I perceive that you believed

This were but woman's weakness, only caused
By this my pain of body, Axel Thordson,
With my left hand I would draw forth my sword,
And challenge you to fight for life and death.

 Axel. I swore by Valborg, that I do respect you.

 Hakon. You swear it. Then you shall esteem
  me too:
For I will make to you a sacrifice.
The sacrifice is great;—'tis needful, Axel!
That you should know its costliness.

 Axel.   My king!

 Hakon. I well know what I hazard by the offer
Of such a gift, at such a time as this:
" Now has the proud and foolish youth at last
Opened his eyes; and now he can perceive
How his throne stands in need of brave defence.
Now does he need his warriors' faithfulness;
And therefore does he purchase friend with maid,
In the despair and anguish of his heart."
Ha,—I would hate you, Axel! I would call you
A cold and cruel and barbarian foe,
If you could dream of such a motive.

 Axel.   Sire

Hakon. For Valborg loses Hakon Norway's realm,
But Valborg— loses he for Valborg's sake.
Think of the value of my gift! Gives one
The greater for the less, to satisfy
One's selfishness?
    Axel.   O Hakon! noble kinsman!
    Hakon. Yes, I have blindly erred, and your pure soul,
Your noble mind, have opened now mine eyes;
And of free-will, because I wish the good,
Do I subdue the passion of my breast,
And give you back your Valborg—give you back
That which to me is dearest in the world.
Misjudge me not,—oh, see my sacrifice!
    Axel. I see it,—and God sees it, noble king!
    Hakon. And now embrace me!
    Axel.   Hold,—your wounded arm!
    Hakon. The wound no longer burns; this linen cloth
Hurts me no more; it cools me, like the juice
Of healing herbs fresh-gathered.
    Axel   O my king!
    Hakon. And now let Erling overcome me. Hakon

Has overcome himself: his victory
Is greatest.

Axel. But it shall not be the last:
The other victory must now be gained.

[*Noise is heard outside the church.*

Be calm, my king! Rest yet a moment longer!
Your golden helm is heavy, and your head
Needs some relief:—give me your helmet. Here,—
Take mine instead; it is a lighter one.

[*The noise increases: Axel throws the king's purple mantle, which has been unloosed during the bandaging, over his own shoulders.*

Hakon. What do you, Axel?

Axel. Nay, be still, my lord!
I hear men coming,—possibly our foes:
Let Axel be a shield to you!

[*A troop of the enemy rushes in.*

The Captain. There stands he!
There stands he! See you? with the golden helmet
And purple robe. It is the king. Rush in—
Rush in on him, and cut him down!

Hakon. O Axel!
Now do I understand your strange behaviour.

Give me my helmet back!

Axel. Nay,—draw your sword,
Place yourself so that your right arm may be
Protected by my body. When you see
An opening, strike,—and then draw back again.
(*He cries.*) Come on, ye paltry wretches! Here stands
　　Hakon.
His sword is drawn, you see: he does not fear
Your coward onslaught in the House of God.
Come on, ye murderers! who do not dare
To stand up man 'gainst man in honest fight,
But think to win base gold by Hakon's murder.
My fiery lion's-tongue is gleaming bright;
Come, let it slake its thirst in traitors' blood!

Hakon (*draws his sword*). He would befool you!
　　Here stands Norway's chief,
And with his left hand will he punish you.

Axel. Peace, Axel Thordson! you are wounded.
　　Hakon
Can well defend himself.

The Enemy. Down with him! down!

　　[*A fight. Noise is heard outside of other
　　warriors: there is a cry—*

To help! to help! The king has been attacked.

The hostile warrior (to Axel). Aha! help comes
too late!   [*He wounds him.*

Haste! flee away!
Hakon is slain! Come on, and cut your way
To Erling through the Biarkebeiners' ranks.
Hakon is slain;—away!

[*Sigurd of Reine and Wilhelm rush in with
a number of Biarkebeiners.*

Sigurd.   Ha, cut and thrust!
Pursue the murderers!

[*The enemy is put to flight.*

Sigurd (to the king). Your life is saved!

[*He becomes aware of Axel.*

What! Axel in the royal robe and helmet?
All bleeding, too?

Axel (to the king). Now take your helm again!
It is too heavy now for *me*. Go, sire!
And leave me with my comrade here alone.

Hakon. My brother! is your wound——

Axel.   Nay,—leave me, king!
Charge boldly on the foe; revenge this treachery;
Follow with Sigurd, and his bark-clad warriors!

Sigurd. Yes, Hakon! even Norway's forests
Have armed themselves to fight for Throndhjem's lord.
Look at these warriors! Gotha-dwellers!* Bears!
Stems of the forest pines, all gathered here
From many a mountain ridge. For want of armour,
This rugged bark protects their gallant hearts.
These stems of alder, with their sharpened points
Hardened by fire, supply the place of spears.
In such wise fight they for their humble hearths,
And the king's honour. Head thou them, my lord,
And by a storm avenge we Axel's slaying.
You die a noble death, my northern brother!
Fallen for your king. We, too, shall follow you
Ere long, perhaps, and greet you before God.
Come, Hakon! Leave him with his friend alone!
Come on!—Life calls for strife, but Death for peace.

Hakon (to his warriors,—pointing at Axel). Ye
Norsemen! for his king he gave his life.

The Biarkebeiners (impatiently strike their wooden spears against the ground). We,—we will also give our lives for thee!

---

* Elvegrimmer, Jal. Elfargrimar, inhabitants of the banks of the Götaelf or Gotha river.

Lead us to death! Lead us against the foe!

Hakon (embraces Axel). Farewell! ere sunset we
shall meet again.

[*He follows the warriors.*

Wilhelm (approaches Axel). My brother! is your
wound a mortal one?

Axel. Yes. Wilhelm! loose my shoulder-scarf, I
pray you!
Draw out the scabbard, and give me the scarf,
That I may stanch the blood a little while,
And respite life. Thanks! Lead me over now
To yonder pillar that bears Valborg's name.
Here shall I rest more easily. So! Let me lean
Against the wall, so that I may not fall
In dying.

Wilhelm. Brother, do you suffer pain?

Axel. No! Light and calm and peaceful is my heart.

Wilhelm. Axel! would you not wish to see your
Valborg
Once more before you die?

Axel. Ah, Wilhelm, yes!

Wilhelm. Then will I hasten up and fetch her
straightway.

Axel. Stay yet a moment! It might happen,
    Wilhelm!
That Axel were no more when Valborg comes.
Then tell the chosen of my heart I died
With Valborg's name upon my lips.
   Wilhelm.   That will I.
   Axel. Tell her, that Hakon is a noble hero;
That Axel's confidence was not misplaced
In trusting to his royal heart.
   Wilhelm.   I will.
   Axel. Greet Helfred,—greet my darling sister,
    Wilhelm!
At Immersborg; and thank her lovingly
For all the thoughts and feelings, joys and sorrows,
She ever shared from childhood with her brother.
Ah, Helfred understood me, knew me well!
Tell her, that I have not forgot my sister
In e'en mine hour of death.
   Wilhelm.   Good! I will greet her.
   Axel. But Valborg first and last! my earnest wish
Is, that whene'er her days on earth are ended,
Axel may slumber by her side.
   Wilhelm.   Your wish

Shall be fulfilled.   Hast more to tell me?

Axel.   Nay!

Wilhelm. Well then,—I go!

Axel (*grasps his hand*).   My noble, faithful
    comrade!
Thanks for your friendship, and your true devotion.
In deeds you showed it, though in words but seldom.
Take from this feeble hand my life's farewell!

Wilhelm. Farewell! Farewell!

Axel.   Wilhelm! was I your friend?

Wilhelm. My only friend! Now have I none
    remaining.   [*He goes.*

Axel (*alone*). I die for land and lord, as did my
    sires.
What honourable Norseman more desires?
O God! with joy my soul doth fly to Thee,
For Thou wilt give the chosen of my heart
To be my bride in Thine eternity,
Where Axel from his Valborg ne'er shall part.

    [*The sun shines through the choir window.*
All hail to thee, thou new-born morning light!
Thou comest to enlighten my dim sight,
And tinge my pallid cheek with thy warm ray.

Soon, soon a morning glow upon me shines,
That never waxes into glaring day;
An evening glow that ne'er to night declines.
My youthful hopes! ye were no shadows vain;—
'Twas mine to love, and to be loved again;
A friend was mine; a noble king God gave,
Whom I have fitted for his station high,
Whom by my death it is my lot to save.—
Well, Axel! thou hast lived, so thou canst die.
And see, my Valborg! yonder angels twine
A wreath of blue Forget-me-nots like thine.
Then thou shalt never from thine Axel part
When thou shalt meet him in those realms above,
More worthy of thy beauty and thine heart,
Where 'tis no sin to nourish sacred love.
Farewell, my Valborg!   [*He dies.*

   Wilhelm (*comes with Valborg*).   He is still alive!
He is alive!   Heard you,—he spoke of Valborg?
   Valborg. I took his life's farewell.
                              [*She gazes on him.*
                              He is no more.—
Mine Axel! dost thou live? If thou dost live,
Lift up on me thine eye for the last time,

Thou noble soul! and let thy blessing shine
On Valborg in thy fixed and dying gaze.
He is no more! Ah, he is dead! He died
With Valborg's name upon his lips. Well, thou
Hast fought thy fight, brave youth! Fell he not for
His king?

   Wilhelm. Ay, as a hero.

   Valborg.   Glorious death!—
Far better this than fly to foreign lands,
To spend thy days in barren banishment,
And waste away with grief of heart, my Axel!
Thou sufferest now no longer, heart-loved youth!
Now hast thou won thyself eternal honour.
Thy Fatherland, thy noble mother Norway,
Is proud of Axel—of her gallant son.
For many an age shall thy belovèd name
Be heard fresh-sounding on her grateful lips;
At Thing-motes men shall often high extol
Thy hero-deed; while in the ladies' bower,
At eventide old ballads shall be sung,
Recounting Axel's love and faithfulness.

                                     [*To Wilhelm.*
How fair he is in death! Thy golden locks

Are wildly scattered round thy pallid brow.

                [*She arranges his hair with her hand.*

So should it be! This brow must not be covered;
'Tis arched so high and noble, like the heavens.
See, how he smiles in death!   [*She kisses him.*

                    Farewell, my Axel!

Thy Valborg follows soon.

    [*She rises up, and lays her hand upon her breast, whilst she draws her breath deeply and heavily.*

                    Ay, soon! ay, soon!

Wilhelm. My noble Valborg! you are pale.

Valborg.   My Axel
Is paler still. Peace, my kind Wilhelm! peace!
Disturb not Valborg in her loneliness.
(*Enthusiastically.*) How pleasant seems it here within
    the church!
How brightly beams the sunshine through the
    windows,
As at this very hour, my Axel! yesterday,
When first thou pressedst Valborg to thy heart.
How homelike 'tis, how cheerful, in the church!
Here shall we live right happily together,

Peacefully dwelling opposite each other,—
Thou with thy father, Valborg with her mother.
And when the clock strikes twelve, and in yon birch
Outside our window sings each night the thrush,—
The wall and marble stones will open wide,
And we shall meet at Harald Gille's grave,
And thence go hand in hand up to the altar,
And sit us down within the moonlit choir,
And let the moon with pale and silv'ry light
Beam on our pallid cheeks, and listen to
The thrush's spring song, whilst we call to mind
The memories of our faithful love in life ;
Then, when the moonlight passes from the choir,
Go back with slow and melancholy steps,
And walk three times round Harald Gille's tomb ;
There shall we pause and take our loving leave
Until the next night comes. Deep in our graves
Then shall we slumber sweetly, whilst the living
Are rioting without.

Wilhelm. And Axel's wish
Was to be buried in one grave with Valborg.

Valborg. In one same grave ? Ah, that were glorious ! But

It may not be, my noble knight! Alas!
Axel and Valborg never were betrothed.
It may not be; yet how much would I give,
That the same coffin might contain both Valborg's
And Axel's bones!—But, noble Wilhelm! Tell me
      [*She gazes down before her.*
What glistens in the dust, in yonder crevice
Of Harald's tombstone?

 Wilhelm.   See I right, it is
A ring.

 Valborg. A ring?

 Wilhelm (*takes it up*). Yes,—it is Axel's ring.

 Valborg. Axel's? Did it not roll into the grave?
Oh, our forefather! now I understand thee:—
I understood thee then. Give me my ring!
      [*She places it upon her finger.*
Now am I truly thy betrothed, my Axel!
Now am I Axel's bride! Now may we be
Buried together in one grave.

 Wilhelm.   Poor girl!

 Valborg. "Poor girl?" Nay, Wilhelm! happy
  happy girl.
Is it not true, my noble friend! I call you

My friend,—for you were Axel Thordson's friend,
Is it not true, my friend! you know the ballad
Of Knight Sir Aage and of Lady Else?

Wilhelm. The Danish bishop taught it to my
mother;
And she, in early childhood, taught it me.

Valborg. And you remember it?

Wilhelm. Yes, perfectly.

Valborg. Oh, that is well! My Axel told me
that
You have a noble voice—not delicate
And soft, like that which pleases men in life;
But deep, and strong, and solemn,—as a voice
From out the grave. Well, noble Wilhelm! will
You show me now the kindness, for the sake
Of him who was your friend, to sing this ballad
For Valborg,—whilst in recompense she places
Her ring upon his cold and lifeless hand?

Wilhelm. Yes, I will do it, if it comforts you.

Valborg. My Axel too has told me, that you are
A skilled musician on the harp.

Wilhelm. Its tones
Full oft have lulled my troubled soul to rest.

Valborg. Well, see in yonder corner, dearest Wilhelm,
Close by my mother's grave, there stands a harp.
How many a sleepless night has Valborg's voice
Risen to its tuneful notes among the tombs!
How many a time has she to it begun
Aage's and Else's ballad! Never yet
I sang it to the end; for hot tears choked
My feeble voice. To you, my noble knight!
To you a stronger nature God has given:
So take the tunèd harp, and sit you down
By yonder pillar, opposite my Axel,
And sing the mournful ballad to the end,
Whilst Valborg kneels beside her Axel's corpse:
And do not rise, I pray, till all is o'er,
And Else is to Aage joined in death.

 Wilhelm. I sing thee comfort in the morning dawn.

  [*Valborg kneels down beside Axel's corpse;
   Wilhelm takes the harp, sits down, and
   sings:—*

   " It was the Knight Sir Aage,
    He rode to the isle his way;
   Wedded he Jomfru Else,
    A fair and goodly May.

Wedded he Jomfru Else,
   All with his ring of gold :
That day a moon thereafter
   Lay he beneath the mould.

"It was the Jomfru Else,
   Her grief could not be told ;
That heard the Knight Sir Aage,
   Deep down beneath the mould.
Up rose the Knight Sir Aage,
   On his back his coffin bore ;
And wending to her bower,
   Scarce could he reach the door.

" He knocked at the door with his coffin,
   Because he had no skin ;—
' Hear thou, Jomfru Else !
   Come, let thy husband in !'
Answered the Jomfru Else,—
   'I open never my door,
Until thou the Holy Name namest,
   As thou usedst to do before.'

" ' Every time thou rejoicest,
   Nor thinkest on thy woes,
Then is it full in my coffin
   With leaves of the red, red rose :

    Every time thou art doleful,
      And at thy heart right sore,
    Then it is full in my coffin
      With red, red clots of gore.

"'The cock is crowing full loudly,
    To the grave must I descend;
To the grave must the dead at cock-crow,
    Their way in silence wend.
Look thou up to the Heaven,
    Up to the star so bright;
Seest thou not how peaceful
    The solemn course of night?'

"Up looked the Jomfru Else,
    Up to the stars so bright;
In his grave sunk down the dead man,
    And vanished rom her sight.
Home went the Jomfru Else,
    Her grief could not be told;
That day a month thereafter
    Lay she beneath the mould."

[*Wilhelm ceases. Valborg lies motionless with her head upon Axel's hand.*

Wilhelm. The song is ended, noble Valborg!

[*He rises.*

Valborg!

Rise up again; my song is ended now.
Valborg! She does not move. Cold, pale! she breathes
No longer. Heaven! I had foreboded it!
Valborg is dead!—As Nanna with her Baldur;
As with her Hjalmar Ingeborg; as Else
With Bidder Aage.—Her true heart has broken
With sorrow o'er the body of her Axel.
O northern faithfulness, how strong thou art!
There lie they both, in one another's arms,
Lifeless,—but now *one* life, *one* soul with God.
And Wilhelm had to sing your funeral dirge!
Well, it was but the tribute due to friendship.

[*Martial music outside the scene.*

Gotfred. (*comes.*) Hakon is fallen: Erling is victorious.
They bring the body of the king.

Wilhelm. And so
The Gille's race is utterly extinct.
Be speedy, Gotfred! Hasten to the bishop;
Take him on board our ship; await me there;
Ere sunset we will sail from Throndhjem's Fjord.

[*The page goes.*

Wilhelm (draws his sword). And now, ye dearest,
    best-belovèd friends!
Until the grave shall open, and unite
What life had parted, shall your Wilhelm show
The honour due by friendship to your dust.
I will keep watch beside you; I will lay
Thy shield and sword, brave knight! upon thy coffin,
Encircled by thy maiden's wreath of flowers;
And on the shining plate will I engrave,
" Here Axel Thordson and fair Valborg rest;
He for his king, she for her lover died."

Miscellaneous Poems.

KING SOLOMON'S DEATH.

(AN ARABIC LEGEND.)

BEFORE his Temple King Solomon stood,
With bowed-down body, in doleful mood;
He knew that his life drew near its close,
And he thought how slowly the walls arose.

King Solomon had a magician's skill,
The spirits of air obeyed his will;
He forced them to bring him treasures untold,—
Jasper and marble, and amber and gold;
Thereof with the quickness of thought arose
A dome which the vault of heaven did enclose:

But though they toiled by day and by night,
It was not yet raised to its destined height.
With hate and ill-will wrought they every hour;
But they dreaded the King and his magic power;
So long as he did in the courtyard stand,
Was no resting a foot, was no resting a hand.
King Solomon had a magician's skill,
But he could not avert Death's power to kill.
His time was come; he should soon be no more;
In his inmost soul it grieved him sore:
Not for his riches and royal state,
Not for his harem's pleasures so great;—
His only, his bitterest, latest care,
Was at leaving God's Temple unfinished there.
He knew that so soon as he should die,
The spirits with scorn and mocking would fly;
Would howl on the winds to distant lands,
"Jerusalem's Temple unfinished stands!"
Then prayed he to God an earnest prayer,—
"I know I must die, and death is fair:
No pleasure is life or glory to me;
Yet my body can never wearied be

So long as there still is wanting alone
To Thy holy Temple one single stone.
Let therefore my body stand, O Lord!
In Thy Temple's court, keeping watch and ward;
Let my gazing eye be a terror still
For many a day to those spirits of ill;
A monument over my grave let me stand
Till in dust this sceptre shall fall from my hand!"

And God let it be as the King did pray;—
The soul released flew to heaven away,
But on earth the body was seen as of yore,
Standing in front of the Temple door.
The right arm was outstretched, with mien of command,
On an ivory sceptre reposed the left hand,
His brow was encircled with golden crown,
From his shoulders a mantle of velvet hung down,
In the wind was waving his hoary hair.
For days and years so stood he there,
And never a moment, by night or by day,
Durst the spirits turn from their work away.

As a worm lay hidden the evil fiend
In the sceptre whereon the body leaned;
And the worm was gnawing by day and night,
While the Temple drew near its destined height.
It gnawed till the sceptre broke at last—
But the crowning stone was laid firm and fast.
The body perished from mortal sight,
But Jerusalem's Temple stood glorious and bright!
For death itself hath not power to kill
The high resolve of an earnest will.

—From the Norwegian of Munch.

DESERTED CHURCH.

There stands an ancient chapel far out upon a reef,
'Mid ocean's raging breakers, where nothing gives relief
To desolation's sternness, where, on the barren stones,
Resounds no human footstep, nought save the salt waves' moans.

The ruined wall sits mourning upon its rock alone;
Within the churchyard, seaweed instead of grass has grown;
Against the shattered windows the bitter sea-foam breaks;
For shelter in the church roof the wearied storm-bird seeks.

The shore is wild and dreary, and on its rugged breast,
It gives to man no refuge, 'tis only death finds rest.
O'er many a stately vessel the billows there have met,
Of the eye of many a seaman the star for ever set.

There was an ancient custom,—how ancient none could know,—
That once in every twelvemonth the priest should thither go,
To preach the holy gospel beside the fallen spire,
The Eucharist to offer within the ruined choir.

'Twas a small congregation—music or song was none;
If some stray fisher sate there, 'twas strange to see that one.
'Mongst empty rows of benches, amid the pillars grey,
Had desolation dire for centuries held sway.

And still, although the church-path lay o'er the treacherous deep,
That ancient pious custom the priest must ever keep;
And though full oft he wished not to cross the boisterous sea,
The people's will, deep rooted, was stronger far than he.

There came into the parish a young priest, who ('twas said)
Was versed in worldly learning, and polished, and well read.

About this yearly voyage he felt but ill at ease,
And to himself soon vowed he,—"This folly now
   shall cease!

"It is full time now surely the land should find relief
From what is still remaining of Popish misbelief;
God's Word should now no longer from man be taken
   more,
And scattered in the tempest upon the barren shore.

"My church stands in the valley, where human beings
   dwell,
Not on yon desert island, where scarce is found a shell.
But once, and for the last time, I go, although full
   loath,
To fetch the sacred volumes and costly altar-cloth!"

It was a cloudy morning when first his foot he set
Upon the rock, with sea-foam glistening, and smooth
   and wet;
The grey mists of the morning the ancient church-
   tower veiled,
The sea-gulls round its turrets in ceaseless circles
   sailed.

The church doors on their hinges, creaked with a
    mournful sound,
But up the long nave quickly, he passed, nor looked
    around :
Through all the broken windows the chilling sea-blast
    swept,
From all the dismal arches re-echoed every step.

"Here 'tis not good to tarry," whispered his lips
    close prest,—
And so spake every feeling within his life-glad
    breast ;—
"Here 'tis not good to tarry, for sons of life not good ;
Another empire's palace for ages here has stood !"

He stood before the altar, whereon the prayer-book
    lay,
In massive silver binding, open for many a day.
He took it from the altar ; the dust rose in a cloud
When in his hand he raised it, while inwardly he
    vowed :—

"So surely as I close these ancient pages now,
No priest shall ever preach here, nor at the altar bow ;

And when I with this volume shall pass through
    yonder door,
Devoted to oblivion be this place for evermore!"

But when the heavy altar book he firmly then did close,
It was as though a death-sigh through all the church
    arose;
And when adown the church-nave he gladly hasted
    straight,
'Twas as though to his footsteps there hung a leaden
    weight.

And when he from the island, light in his boat did
    glide,
'Twas as though from the billows the voice of children
    cried;
A deep low sound of wailing far o'er the ocean flies,—
From men who suffer shipwreck it seems to him to
    rise.

But to the winds he quickly cast all these thoughts of
    fear,
When home's green fields lay smiling in sunshine,
    once more near:

He boasted of his victory, and ridiculed his fright,
When in his peaceful dwelling he sate e'er close of
  night.

A year had passed already,—it was the self-same day;
His friends were gathered round him, so cheerful and
  so gay.
He cried across the table,—"'Tis better here to be,
Than in that empty chapel far out amid the sea."

That evening he was sitting, after the day was spent,
Within his quiet study, and thinking, well-content,—
"That stupid superstition I have now made to cease;
'Tis dead, and shall not trouble henceforward more
  my peace."

So mused he; but while turning the page he read, a cold,
Involuntary shudder came o'er him as of old:
He felt that he no longer was solitary here,
Some strange mysterious being he felt was standing
  near.

He started, and then gazing towards a gloomy nook,
It was as though the darkness some shape and like-
  ness took;

It gathered form and substance, drew near, and slowly
    turned,
And now a human image with terror he discerned.

An aged bent-down sailor he thought that he could
    see,
Beaten by wind and weather, pale as death's agony;
And still the salt sea-water from hair and clothes did
    flow;
His hands were clenched together, as in the utmost woe.

And yet no sign of terror lay on that pallid face,
Unutterable sorrow alone had left its trace;
And from that eye deep-sunken went forth a silent
    prayer;
Most deep, most earnest longing, was lying hidden
    there.

Then stood it still before him, and silent as the
    tomb,
Like a mirror's dim reflection in a half-darkened
    room.
He strove to rise in terror, a shriek lay on his tongue;
But leaden-weighted palsy to all his members clung.

Then marked he that the spectre, as though it fain
 would speak,
Its pale lips slowly opened, though no words the
 silence break ;
But in his inmost being, deep where the soul doth
 dwell,
Strange echoes were awakened, as by a magic spell :—

" Whence I am come thou knowest; evening has past
 away,
And thy poor congregation awaits thee all the day.
Alone thou wast not ever in yonder house of prayer ;
A reverent assembly was gathered round thee there.

" For all who there have perished in the wild tempest's
 shock,
The dying thought their spirits binds to that lone sea-
 girt rock.
'Twixt day and night to wander is there our weary lot,
Alike of earth and heaven forsaken and forgot.

" To pray we are not able ; but life's strong voice can
 cheer
With Jesus' holy comfort our souls oppressed with fear ;

When prayer and praise are sounding over the ocean wave,
The light of far redemption dawns on our darksome grave.

"So thought long since a Christian; he built yon sacred pile
In aid of souls departed upon the desert isle.
Through years and generations has stood his pious will,
Thy ancient fathers' custom, why wilt not thou fulfil?

"That single brief hour only, to us each year did bring;
Thou all life's days possessest, in its summer and its spring.
Give us then of thy riches, and when they pass from thee,
Thou shalt not pine with longing and bitter ruth, as we."

Past is the ghastly vision, but he finds no relief;
His troubled soul turns straightway from doubt to firm belief.

L

That night outweighed a lifetime. At early dawn of day
Still in his arm-chair sleepless and pale and wan he lay.

In all his friends came rushing; but they started, struck with awe,
When in those haggard features a countenance they saw
Whereon was still remaining a reflection of the light
From the spirit world that lately had opened on his sight.

He rose up calm and solemn: "Depart in peace!" (he said);
"Thither ye cannot follow where now my steps are led."
He took the sacred vestments, the surplice and the cope,
And to the island sailed he, but never word he spoke.

He left his boatmen standing behind him on the shore;
They watched, and saw him slowly enter the church's door.

They saw the massive church doors after him straightway close,
Within what may have happened, he never would disclose.

But deeply changed in spirit became he from that day;
A smile was no more ever seen upon his lips to play.
In winter and in summer, in calm or tempest's rage,
He never more neglected his silent pilgrimage.

He heard the scorn and laughter of the worldly and the gay,—
And yet it was not therefore his hair grew early grey;
But one might hear him often, sighing in grief of heart,—
" Believers who have seen not—their's is the blessed part!"

—From the Norwegian of Munch.

TO * * * * *

When down the stream the swan is softly gliding,
    Then think I, O my silent friend! on thee,
And on the dream thou in thy soul art hiding,
    But which one day thou wilt confide to me.

When in the sky the fires of night are gleaming,
    Then think I, O my hidden hope! on thee,
And on the fire that from thine eye is beaming,
    And on the glance that hath enraptured me.

The pallid moon is rising while day faileth,
    So riseth too my longing after thee:
Now onward, like a phantom ship, she saileth,
    Ah! think I, hath death power to rescue me?

For gladly would I die before the morrow,
    If in the grave I should recover thee;
But heaven itself would be a house of sorrow,
    If thou wert not united there with me."

— From the Danish of Professor Hauch.

THE END.

www.ingramcontent.com/pod-product-compliance
Lightning Source LLC
Chambersburg PA
CBHW031448160426
43195CB00010BB/901